What's the
Matter?

a physical science unit for high-ability learners in grades 2–3

What's the Matter?

A Project Clarion Science Unit for Primary Grades
Funded by the Jacob K. Javits Program, United States Department of Education

The College of William and Mary
School of Education
Center for Gifted Education
P.O. Box 8795
Williamsburg, VA 23187-8795

Co-Principal Investigators: Bruce A. Bracken, Ph.D., and Joyce VanTassel-Baska, Ed.D.
Project Managers: Tamra Stambaugh, Ph.D., Janice Robbins, Ph.D., Valerie Gregory, Ed.D.
Unit Developers: Ellen Fithian, Ph.D., Tamra Stambaugh, Ph.D., and Peggy Jaquot
Revised by: Elizabeth B. Sutton

Edited by Lacy Elwood
Production Design by Marjorie Parker

ISBN-13: 978-1-59363-328-8
ISBN-10: 1-59363-328-9

Prufrock Press Inc.
P.O. Box 8813
Waco, TX 76714-8813
Phone: (800) 998-2208
Fax: (800) 240-0333
http://www.prufrock.com

Contents

Part I: Unit Overview

Introduction to the Unit

The Project Clarion Science Units for Primary Grades are designed to introduce young students to science concepts and science processes. These units utilize a hands-on, constructivist approach that allows children to build their knowledge base and their skills as they explore science topics through play and planned investigations. Students are engaged in creative and critical thinking, problem finding and solving, process skill development, and communication opportunities. Each individual unit is designed to strengthen essential concepts such as quantity, direction, position, comparison, colors, letter identification, numbers, counting, size, social awareness, texture, material, shape, time, and sequence. The Project Clarion Science Units for Primary Grades also focus on overarching concepts such as systems, change, and cause and effect.

What's the Matter? is a physical science unit for high-ability learners in grades 2–3 that focuses on the properties of solids, liquids, gases, and the processes by which matter changes states. In this unit, students work on problem-solving scenarios that utilize their new knowledge of matter, change in physical properties, and the measurement of matter—all while preparing a presentation to share new ideas and discoveries about matter in a classroom Matter Conference. The overarching concept of *change* is incorporated within the lessons to deepen students' understanding of the scientific concepts in this unit.

Essential Understandings of the Unit

Through completion of this unit, the student will convey the following essential understandings:
- All common substances are made of matter.
- Matter is anything that has mass and takes up space.
- There are three main states of matter: solids, liquids, and gases.
- Objects can be described by color, shape, texture, relative size and weight, and position.
- Matter can change from one state to another; these changes are referred to as physical changes.
- Volume is the measure of the amount of space occupied by matter.
- Mass is a measure of the amount of matter.
- Materials are composed of parts that are too small to see without magnification.
- Physical properties remain the same when a material is reduced in size.
- Some liquids separate when mixed with water.
- Some solids will dissolve in water, and more quickly in hot than cold water.
- Temperature and energy can create physical changes in matter.

Before you begin, you may choose to use the preteaching lesson on safety in the science classroom, Science Safety (pp. 23–26). Simulating the work of real scientists, students develop a systematic set of inquiry skills. As scientists, students must learn the basic safety precautions that are necessary while performing experiments of different nature. Science safety is outlined in a brief lesson that is located prior to the preassessment lesson. This optional lesson is designed to outline the science safety rules in this unit, as well as to instill in students the importance of safety in the classroom. Science safety guidelines for teachers also are provided in this lesson.

Scientific Investigation and Reasoning

The Wheel of Scientific Investigation and Reasoning contains the specific processes involved in scientific inquiry that guide students' thinking and actions. To read more about these processes and suggestions for implementing the wheel into this unit's lessons, see Appendix A: Teaching Models (pp. 141–151).

The following lessons heavily utilize the Wheel of Scientific Investigation and Reasoning: Lesson 2 helps students to gain a better understanding of what scientists do; Lesson 4 introduces the wheel, including the six components of scientific investigation; and Lesson 5 continues the introduction to scientific investigation by requiring students to make observations, ask questions, learn more about the topic, design and conduct experiments, and share their results.

Students apply the components of scientific investigation throughout this unit by using the wheel to analyze aspects of an investigation and for planning investigations. Concepts of scientific reasoning and investigation within the lessons include:

- To make observations, scientists use their senses, as well as instruments, to note details, identify similarities and differences, and record changes in phenomena.
- Observations about familiar objects or events often lead to the development of important questions that can spark further investigation.
- Investigation requires a careful review of what is known and what additional information must be sought.
- An experiment is a fair test designed to answer a question.
- Scientific investigations require careful gathering and analysis of data.
- To communicate findings, one must provide a clear description of what question was asked, what prediction was made, what experiment was conducted, what data were collected and analyzed, and what conclusions and inferences were developed.

Concepts Covered in This Unit

Many teachers find concept mapping useful for envisioning the scope of a lesson or unit. Teachers also use student-developed concept maps as a way of measuring student progress. Each Project Clarion unit contains an overview concept map (see Figure 1) that displays the essential knowledge included in the lessons and the connections students should be able to make as a result of their experiences within the unit. This overview may be useful as a classroom poster that teachers and students can refer to throughout the unit.

Practice in using concept maps supports students' learning as they begin to build upon known concepts. Students begin to add new concepts to their initial understanding of a topic and to make new connections between concepts. The use of concept maps within the lessons also helps teachers to recognize students' conceptual frameworks so that instruction can be adapted as necessary. More information on strategies for using concept mapping, as well as a list of concept mapping practice activities, are provided in Appendix A: Teaching Models.

Overarching Concept

The overarching concept for this unit is *change*. The natural world changes continually; however, some changes may be too slow to observe. Students will begin to understand the concept of change in science by learning about natural changes that occur over time, as well as manmade changes that impact conditions. Change

4

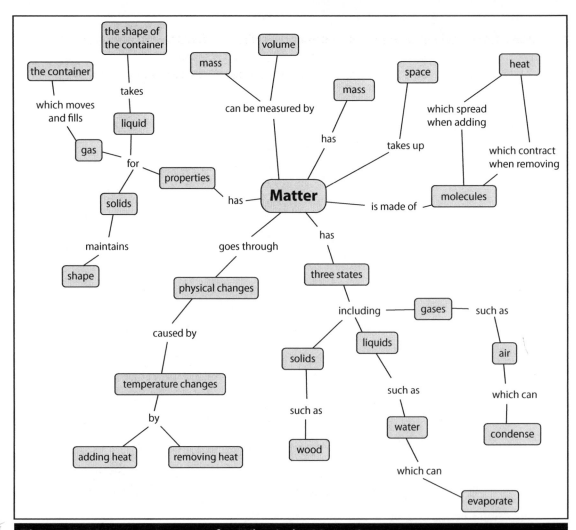

Figure 1. Unit concept map for *What's the Matter?*

was chosen with reference to the concepts selected by Rutherford and Ahlgren in *Science for All Americans* (1990), those selected by the writers of the California Science Framework, and those selected by Judson for his book *The Search for Solutions* (1980). Additional criteria applied to selecting the concept were: (1) ease of applicability to all science areas, (2) numerous valid connections to nonscience domains of inquiry, and (3) nature of being highly workable to demonstrate content manifestations at the unit level of analysis.

The first lesson in this unit introduces the concept of change. (This lesson is based on Taba's Model of Concept Development; for more on this model, see Appendix A.) Students are asked to brainstorm examples of change, categorize their examples, identify nonexamples of the concept, and make generalizations about the concept. The following generalizations about change are incorporated into this unit of study:

- Change is everywhere.
- Change relates to time.
- Change can be natural or manmade.
- Change may be random or predictable.

Change is integrated throughout this unit's lessons, adding depth to students' understanding of matter and how the physical states of matter may change. Students examine the relationship of important ideas, abstractions, and issues through the application of the concept generalizations. For example, the "Concluding Questions and/or Actions" section of each lesson plan often includes a question that specifically addresses select change generalizations and requires students to make applications to essential science understandings. This higher level thinking enhances students' ability to "think like a scientist." Teachers should assess students' ability to apply the concept of change by seeking evidence that students:

- understand that change is everywhere,
- demonstrate the impact of time on change,
- articulate the nature of natural vs. manmade changes,
- evaluate the nature of change in selected phenomena, and
- articulate the differences between random and predictable changes.

To learn more about the implementation of concept development to the lesson plans, please read the extensive guide located in Appendix A.

Curriculum Framework

The curriculum framework (see Table 1) developed for the Project Clarion science units is based on the Integrated Curriculum Model (ICM), which posits the relatively equal importance of teaching to high-level content, higher order processes and resultant products, and important concepts and issues. The model represents a merger between the new curriculum reform agenda and key approaches found appropriate for high-ability learners. The framework serves several important functions:

1. The curriculum framework provides scaffolding for the central concept of change, the scientific research process, and the content of the units.
2. The curriculum framework also provides representative statements of advanced, complex, and sophisticated learner outcomes. It demonstrates how a single set of outcomes for all can be translated appropriately for high-ability learners, yet remain accessible to other learners.
3. The curriculum framework provides a way for readers to get a snapshot view of the key emphases of the curriculum in direct relation to each other. The model also provides a way to traverse the elements individually through the continuum of grade levels.

Moreover the framework may be used to implement the William and Mary units and to aid in new curriculum development based on science reform recommendations.

Standards Met

Table 2 presents detailed information on how the lessons in this unit align to the National Science Education Standards.

Assessment

What's the Matter? contains performance-based assessments for students to complete at the beginning (preassessment) and end (postassessment) of the unit to assess learning within the unit itself. These assessments address concept attainment, scientific process and/or investigation, and unit content. Teachers should use the performance-based assessment results from the preassessment (pp. 27–35) to adjust instructional plans for individual learners as needed. The preassessment results also provide a baseline for determining growth after the postassessment (pp. 131–139) is administered at the completion of the unit. The postassessment

Table 1
Curriculum Framework for
Project Clarion Science Units for Primary Grades

Goal	Student Outcomes The student will be able to:
1. Develop selected basic concepts in 11 categories (color, letter identification, numbers/counting, sizes, comparisons, shapes, direction/position, self-/social awareness, texture/material, quantity, time/sequence), related to understanding the world of science and mathematics.	• Provide examples, illustrations, and salient features of important science/math concepts. • Categorize and/or classify various concepts. • Identify counterexamples of specific concepts. • Create definitions and generalizations about individual, basic concepts.
2. Develop an understanding of the concept of change as it relates to science content goals.	• Provide examples of changes everywhere. • Demonstrate or identify the impact of time on change. • Categorize examples of natural changes and manmade changes. • Evaluate the nature of change in selected phenomena. • Analyze orderly changes and random changes.
3. Develop knowledge of selected content topics in science and mathematics.	• Understand that common substances are made of matter. • Define matter as anything that has mass and takes up space. • Identify three main states of matter: solids, liquids, and gases. • Describe objects by color, shape, texture, relative size and weight, and position. • Determine physical changes in matter. • Use volume to measure of the amount of space occupied by matter. • Use mass to measure of the amount of matter. • Conclude that materials are composed of parts that are too small to see without magnification. • Analyze how physical properties remain the same when a material is reduced in size. • Articulate that some liquids separate when mixed with water. • Note that solids will dissolve in water, and some will dissolve more quickly in hot than cold water. • Apply temperature and energy to create physical changes in matter.
4. Develop interrelated science process skills.	• Make observations. • Ask questions. • Learn more. • Design and conduct the experiment. • Create meaning from the experiment. • Tell others what was found.
5. Develop critical thinking skills.	• Describe problematic situations or issues. • Define relevant concepts. • Identify different points of view in situations or issues. • Describe evidence or data supporting a point of view in a situation or issue. • Draw conclusions based on data (inferencing). • Predict consequences.
6. Develop creative thinking skills.	• Develop fluency when naming objects and ideas, based on a stimulus. • Develop flexible thinking. • Elaborate on ideas presented in oral or written form. • Create products that replicate and extend conceptual understanding.
7. Develop curiosity and interest in the world of science.	• Express reactions about discrepant events. • Ask meaningful questions about science topics. • Articulate ideas of interest about science. • Demonstrate persistence in completing science tasks.

Table 2
What's the Matter Unit: Alignment to National Science Education Standards

Standard	Fundamental Concepts	Unit Lessons
Content Standard A: Science as Inquiry.	Abilities necessary to do scientific inquiry: • Ask a question about objects, organisms, and events in the environment. • Plan and conduct a simple investigation. • Employ simple equipment and tools to gather data and extend the senses. • Use data to construct a reasonable explanation. • Communicate investigations and explanations.	1, 2, 3, 4, 5, 6, 7, 8, 9, 10, 11, 12, 13, 14, 15
	Understanding about scientific inquiry: • Scientific investigations involve asking questions and answering with what scientists already know about the world. • Scientists use different kinds of investigations depending on the questions they are trying to answer. Types of investigations include describing objects, events, and organisms; classifying them; and doing a fair test (experimenting). • Simple instruments such as magnifiers, thermometers, and rulers provide more information than scientists obtain using only their senses. • Scientists develop explanations using observations (evidence) and what they already know about the world (scientific knowledge). Good explanations are based on evidence from investigations. • Scientists report the results of their investigations in ways that enable others to repeat the investigations. • Scientists review and ask questions about the results of other scientists' work.	1, 2, 3, 4, 5, 6, 7, 8, 9, 10, 11, 12, 13, 14, 15
Content Standard B: Physical Science.	Properties of objects and materials: • Objects have many observable properties, including size, weight, shape, color, temperature, and the ability to react with other substances. Those properties can be measured using tools such as rulers, balances, and thermometers. • Materials can exist in different states: solids, liquids, and gases. Some common materials such as water can be changed from one state to another by heating or cooling.	3, 6, 7, 8, 9, 10, 11, 12, 13, 15
Content Standard E: Science and Technology.	Abilities of technological design: • Identify a simple problem. • Propose a solution. • Implement proposed solutions. • Evaluate a product or design. • Communicate a problem, design, and solution.	6, 10, 14
	Understanding about science and technology: • Tools help scientists make better observations, measurements, and equipment for investigations. They help scientists to see, measure, and do things that they could not otherwise see, measure, and do.	9, 10, 11

provides valuable information about students' mastery of the targeted objectives and National Science Education Standards.

Within both the pre- and postassessment, the following exercises are used in order to assess students' knowledge:

- The Preassessment for Change Concept (pp. 28–30) on the overarching concept, change, is administered prior to the first lesson. Students then are given assessment templates where they are asked to draw or write about certain changes. A concept assessment rubric is used to score the concept pre- and postassessments.

- In the Preassessment for Scientific Process (pp. 31–33), students are given a scientific question and are asked to design an experiment to investigate the question. A response template is given to students, and this template prompts them to identify a prediction or hypothesis, materials needed for the experiment, experiment steps, data collection, and data organization for interpretation. The rubrics are used to assess students' responses to the prompts.
- Concept maps are used to pre- and postassess students' knowledge of matter. Prior to the preassessment, students should have experience in creating concept maps to represent their knowledge (see Concept Mapping Overview in Appendix A). At the time of the actual preassessment, students are given a prompt for creating a concept map about matter. After completion, students' maps are awarded a specific number of points for hierarchical levels, propositions, cross-connections, and examples.

Teachers also should note that assessment "Look Fors" are designated in the first section of each lesson plan. These are linked to the essential science understandings, scientific processes, and change concept generalizations that are targeted in each lesson. Teachers can develop checklists for the "Look Fors" or may make informal assessment observations.

In addition to these assessment tools, teachers also will notice references to a "word wall" in the unit. The word wall is suggested for use in the classroom while teaching the unit. On this wall, teachers will post or write words (and their definitions) that go along with the lessons. Use the definitions listed on the Unit Glossary (p. 10) for the word wall. In each Materials/Resources/Equipment section of a lesson, teachers will be given words to add to the word wall that correspond to the concepts in each lesson. Then, at the end of the unit, teachers are instructed to assign words from the word wall to student groups for an activity that involves students creating word demonstrations. Teachers can assess students' understanding of each word or concept by the quality of understanding demonstrated in students' presentations.

Unit Glossary

boiling point: the temperature at which all of the particles of a liquid have enough energy to turn into vapor (or gas)

chemical change: a change in matter whereby it is turned into a different type of matter

condensation: the process by which a gas changes into a liquid

displace: to take the place of something

dissolve: break apart by placing a solid into a liquid

energy: power from coal, electricity, or other sources that makes machines work and produces heat

evaporation: the vaporization of the surface particles of a liquid when the liquid is not hot enough to boil

experiment: a scientific test to try out a theory or to see the effect of something

freezing point: the temperature at which a liquid turns solid or freezes

gas: a substance, such as air, that will spread to fill any space that contains it

graduated container: a container that has lines on the side that allow for measurement of the volume of liquid in it

hypothesis: a temporary prediction that can be tested about how a scientific investigation or experiment will turn out

infer: to draw a conclusion after considering all of the facts

investigation: if you investigate something, you find out as much as possible about it

liquid: a wet substance you can pour

mass: a measure of how much matter there is in an object

matter: anything that has a physical presence, that has mass and takes up space

melting point: the temperature at which a solid changes into a liquid

molecule: the smallest part of a substance that displays all of the chemical properties of that substance; a molecule is made up of more than one atom

observation: the careful watching of someone or something

physical change: a change in the physical properties of matter that does not change matter into a different type of matter

predict: to say what you think will happen in the future

property: a characteristic of matter, such as its color, shape, texture, or temperature

scientist: a person who studies nature and the physical world by testing, experimenting, and measuring

solid: hard and firm; not a liquid or a gas

solution: a mixture made up of a substance that has been dissolved in a liquid

state: as in states of matter: the way that something is, or the condition it is in

volume: the amount of space that an object takes up

water vapor: the gas produced when water evaporates

Teacher Content Notes

States of Matter

All matter is made up of small particles called *atoms*. Different arrangements of atoms have different properties. Tightly compressed groups of atoms with little space between them make solid objects, whereas widely spaced groups of atoms make liquids or gasses. Atoms combine to make molecules. Solid, liquid, and gas are known as the three states of matter, although plasma now is considered a fourth state. Plasma exists at very high temperatures, and molecules in that state can behave very differently. Plasma does not naturally occur on earth because of the very high temperatures that are required. Plasma is ionized gas that is composed of free-moving electrons and ions. Ions are atoms that have lost electrons. Because a great deal of power is needed to separate electrons from their atoms, plasma is very rare on earth. It sometimes is found in small concentration around lightning. Plasma exists in greater concentrations in space, and the sun and stars are comprised of plasma.

Each state has certain properties. A solid object keeps its shape regardless of where it is placed, is difficult to move through, and cannot be compressed. A liquid takes the shape of its container, can be moved through or poured, and only can be compressed with difficulty. A gas expands to fill its container and can be moved through and compressed easily.

Substances can move from one state to another at various temperatures. Water, for instance, has a solid form (ice), a liquid form (water), and a gaseous form (water vapor). A substance changes from solid to liquid when it reaches its melting point, from liquid to gas when it reaches it boiling point, from liquid to solid when it reaches its freezing point, and from gas to liquid when it reaches its condensation point. The melting and freezing points of any substance are the same, as are the boiling and condensation points. For water, the freezing (and melting) point is 32°F, and the boiling (and condensation) point is 212°F. If a substance is placed under extreme pressure, its boiling and freezing points will change. Heat is the energy transferred as part of the temperature change. Heat is either added or taken away from a substance in order for it to change states from or to freezing or boiling.

Mass, Volume, and Density

An object's mass is the amount of matter it contains. Mass is measured on a balance or scale in units like grams and kilograms. Volume is the amount of space filled by an object. The volume of a solid can be measured using its dimensions; in other words, the volume of a rectangular box 1 foot long, 2 feet wide, and 3 feet high would be 6 cubic feet ($V = L \times W \times H$). To measure the volume of a liquid, pour it into a graduated container (a container labeled with incremental measurements). The volume of a liquid is measured using units such as milliliters and gallons. An object can have both a high (or low) mass and a high (or low) volume, or it can have a high mass and low volume or low volume and high mass. Think, for instance, of balls. A ping-pong ball has both low mass and low volume. A golf ball has a higher mass, but a similar low volume. A medicine ball has a high mass and volume, while a beach ball has a low mass but high volume.

The ratio between an object's matter and volume is its density. In other words, density equals mass divided by volume. An object with a high density will have less volume than an equal mass of a less dense object. For example, a one-pound bag of feathers has a greater volume than a one-pound block of steel because the steel has the greater density.

A compound's density can be changed by changing its temperature. When a compound is heated, its atoms spread out and it expands. Because it now is taking up more volume with the same mass, its density is lower. When the compound cools and the atoms contract, it will take up less volume and its density will increase. Lava lamps work on this principle. Two substances of similar densities that will not mix together are put in the lamp. As one substance comes in contact with the lamp's heat source, it warms up and expands. Because it now is less dense than the surrounding substance, it rises to the top of the lamp. When the substance reaches the top of the lamp, it cools down, becomes denser, and sinks to the bottom. This is how the changing patterns inside the lamp are created.

Teaching Resources

Required Resources

Lehn, B. (1998). *What is a scientist?* Brookfield, CT: The Millbrook Press.

Additional Resources

Adler, D. (1999). *How tall, how short, how faraway?* New York: Holiday House.

Ansary, M. T. (1997). *Matter.* Crystal Lake, IL: Rigby Education.

Clark, J. O. E. (2001). *Physics matters! Volume 1: Matter.* Danbury, CT: Grolier Educational.

Cobb, V. (1990). *Why can't you unscramble an egg? And other not such dumb questions about matter.* Dutton, NY: Lodestar Books.

Curry, D. L. (2004). *What is mass?* New York: Scholastic.

Fiarotta, N., & Fiarotta, P. (1997). *Great experiments with H_2O.* New York: Sterling.

Frost, H. (2000). *Water as a gas.* Mankato, MN: Pebble Books.

Fullick, A. (1999). *Matter.* Chicago: Heinemann Library.

Gardner, R. (2000). *Science projects about methods of measuring.* Berkeley Heights, NJ: Enslow.

Gardner, R. (2003). *Super-sized science projects with volume: How much space does it take up?* Berkeley Heights, NJ: Enslow.

Jennings, T. (1989). *Balancing.* New York: Gloucester Press.

Knapp, B. (2003). *Changing from solids to liquids to gases.* Danbury, CT: Grolier Educational.

Leedy, L. (1997). *Measuring Penny.* New York: Henry Holt & Co.

Markle, S. (1995). *Measuring up! Experiments, puzzles, and games exploring measurement.* New York: Aladdin Paperbacks.

Mellett, P. (2001). *Matter and materials.* New York: Kingfisher.

Ontario Science Center. (1995). *Starting with science: Solids, liquids, and gases.* Toronto, ON: Author.

Oxlade, C. (1999). *Energy.* Des Plaines, IL: Heinemann Library.

Patilla, P. (2000). *Measuring.* Des Plaines, IL: Heinemann Library

Schwartz, M. (2003). *Millions to measure.* New York: HarperCollins.

Tocci, S. (2001). *Experiments with solids, liquids, and gases.* New York: Scholastic.

Trumbauer, L. (2004). *What are atoms?* New York: Scholastic.

Trumbauer, L. (2006). *What is volume?* New York: Scholastic.

Wick, W. (1997). *A drop of water.* New York: Scholastic.

Zoehfeld, K. W. (1998). *What is the world made of? All about solids, liquids, and gases.* New York: HarperCollins.

Useful Web Sites

Rader's Chem4Kids
http://www.chem4kids.com

NASA's Kids Science News Network
http://ksnn.larc.nasa.gov/k2/k2_science.html
http://ksnn.larc.nasa.gov/k2/s_statesMatter_v.html

Science for All
http://www.scienceforall.com

National Institute of Science and Technology: Taking America's Measure
http://www.nist.gov/public_affairs/kids/kidsmain.htm

Part II: Lesson Plans

Lesson Plans

Lesson Plan Overview

Lesson 1—What Is Change?

Lesson 2—What Is a Scientist?

Lesson 3—Introduction to Matter

Lesson 4—What Scientists Do: Observe, Question, Learn More

Lesson 5—What Scientists Do: Experiment, Create Meaning, Tell Others

Lesson 6—The Case of the Mystery Goop

Lesson 7—Physical Changes by Changing Temperatures

Lesson 8—Who Stole the Principal's Water?

Lesson 9—Who Stole the Principal's Water? Part II

Lesson 10—Measuring Mass

Lesson 11—Measuring Volume

Lesson 12—Evaporation Findings

Lesson 13—Condensation

Lesson 14—Planning the Investigation and Hosting the Matter Conference

Lesson 15—Concluding the Unit

Lesson Overview

The following pages provide organizational tools you can use with the lessons provided in this book.

Unit Flowchart

The lessons in this book were designed with a particular organizational system of presenting the information in mind. Figure 2 presents a flowchart we have designed for conducting the various lessons in this unit.

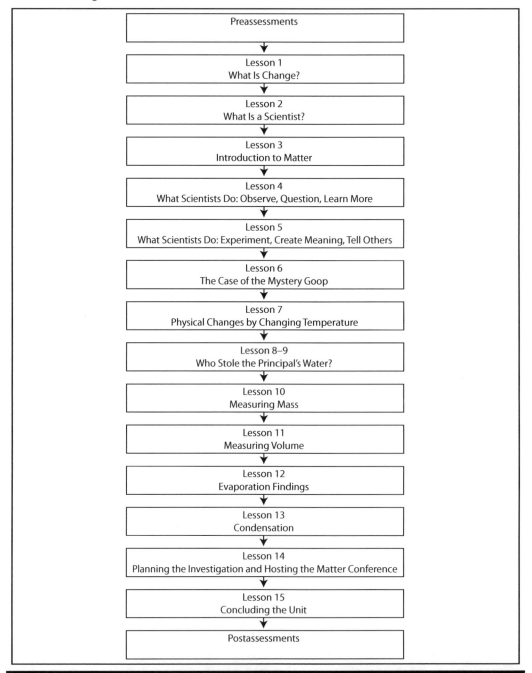

Preassessments

↓

Lesson 1
What Is Change?

↓

Lesson 2
What Is a Scientist?

↓

Lesson 3
Introduction to Matter

↓

Lesson 4
What Scientists Do: Observe, Question, Learn More

↓

Lesson 5
What Scientists Do: Experiment, Create Meaning, Tell Others

↓

Lesson 6
The Case of the Mystery Goop

↓

Lesson 7
Physical Changes by Changing Temperature

↓

Lesson 8–9
Who Stole the Principal's Water?

↓

Lesson 10
Measuring Mass

↓

Lesson 11
Measuring Volume

↓

Lesson 12
Evaporation Findings

↓

Lesson 13
Condensation

↓

Lesson 14
Planning the Investigation and Hosting the Matter Conference

↓

Lesson 15
Concluding the Unit

↓

Postassessments

Figure 2. *What's the Matter?* unit flowchart.

Lesson Plan Blueprint

In planning to incorporate these lessons in your classroom, you might find the blueprint included in Table 3 handy. This table breaks down each lesson, detailing the instructional purpose, essential science understandings, scientific investigation skills and processes, generalizations about the overarching concept of change, and the basic concepts emphasized in the unit.

Table 3
Lesson Plan Blueprint

Lesson #	Title	Instructional Purpose	Essential Science Understandings	Scientific Investigation Skills and Processes	Change Generalizations
	Preassessments				
1	What Is Change?	To understand the concept of change and apply change generalizations.	• Some liquids separate when mixed with water.		• Change is everywhere. • Change is related to time. • Change can be natural or manmade. • Change can be random or predictable.
2	What Is a Scientist?	To analyze characteristics of scientists and to learn about investigation skills that scientists use.		• Make observations. • Ask questions. • Learn more about observations and questions. • Design and conduct experiments. • Create meaning from the experiment. • Tell others what was found.	
3	Introduction to Matter	To identify, observe, and investigate a scenario—the properties of the three states of matter.	• All common substances are made of matter. • Matter is anything that has mass and takes up space. • There are three states of matter: solids, liquids, and gases. • Objects can be described by color, shape, texture, relative size and weight, and position.	• Make observations. • Collect, classify, and analyze data. • Communicate findings.	
4	What Scientists Do: Observe, Question, Learn More	To apply the Wheel of Scientific Investigation and Reasoning (make observations, ask questions, and learn more) to investigate gas in opened and unopened bottles of soda pop.	• Objects can be described by color, shape, texture, relative size, weight, and position. • There are three states of matter: solids, liquids, and gases. • Physical properties remain the same when a material changes in size.	• Make observations. • Ask questions. • Learn more about observations and questions.	
5	What Scientists Do: Experiment, Create Meaning, Tell Others	To design and conduct an experiment about what happens to the properties of matter when reduced in size, create meaning from the experiment, and tell others what was found. To understand what the scenario is asking students to do.	• Objects can be described by color, shape, texture, relative size and weight, and position. • Physical properties remain the same when a material changes in size.	• Design and conduct experiments. • Create meaning from the experiment. • Tell others what was found.	• Change can be natural or manmade. • Change can be random or predictable.

Lesson #	Title	Instructional Purpose	Essential Science Understandings	Scientific Investigation Skills and Processes	Change Generalizations
6	The Case of the Mystery Goop	To understand the concept of molecules and how they act in solids, liquids, and gases. To investigate whether a mystery substance is a solid or a liquid based on the properties of matter and how molecules in matter are combined.	• Matter is anything that has mass and takes up space. • There are three states of matter: solids, liquids, and gases. • Materials are composed of parts that are too small to see without magnification.	• Observe. • Ask questions. • Learn more. • Tell others what was found. • Make predictions.	• Change may be random or predictable. • Change is everywhere. • Change may happen naturally or be caused by people.
7	Physical Changes by Changing Temperature	To analyze the physical states of matter and the importance of removing or adding heat as part of the physical change. To make ice cream to demonstrate removal of heat in a change of matter.	• Matter is anything that has mass and takes up space. • Matter can change from one state to another; these changes are referred to as physical changes. • Temperature and energy can create physical changes in matter. • Materials are composed of parts that are too small to see without magnification.	• Draw inferences. • Communicate findings.	• Change is related to time. • Change can be natural or caused by people.
8	Who Stole the Principal's Water?	To examine and investigate the importance of temperature on the molecules of solids, liquids, and gases. To understand evaporation by trying to figure out what happened to salt water in the principal's office.	• Matter is anything that has mass and takes up space. • Matter can change from one state to another; these changes are referred to as physical changes. • Temperature and energy can create physical changes in matter. • Materials are composed of parts that are too small to see without magnification.	• Make observations. • Ask questions. • Learn more about observations and questions.	
9	Who Stole the Principal's Water? Part II	To investigate who stole the principal's ocean water based on what was learned from the previous lesson. To begin planning an independent investigation on matter for the matter conference.	• Matter is anything that has mass and takes up space. • Matter can change from one state to another; these changes are referred to as physical changes. • Temperature and energy can create physical changes in matter. • Materials are composed of parts that are too small to see without magnification. • Some solids will dissolve in water, and more quickly in hot than cold water.	• Make observations. • Ask questions. • Learn more about observations and questions. • Design and conduct experiments. • Create meaning from the experiment. • Tell others what was found.	• Change is everywhere.
10	Measuring Mass	To measure the mass of matter in solids and liquids by using a balance. To conduct a simple investigation to determine if the mass of an ice cube stays the same when it melts.	• Mass is a measure of the amount of matter. • There are three states of matter: solids, liquids, and gases. • All common substances are made of matter. • Matter is anything that has mass and takes up space. • Matter can change from one state to another; these changes are referred to as physical changes.	• Make observations. • Ask questions. • Learn more about observations and questions. • Design and conduct experiments. • Create meaning from experiments. • Tell others what was found.	• Change is linked to time. • Change can be natural or manmade. • Change can be random or predictable. • Change is everywhere.

Lesson #	Title	Instructional Purpose	Essential Science Understandings	Scientific Investigation Skills and Processes	Change Generalizations
11	Measuring Volume	To measure the volume of two types of matter: solids and liquids.	• Matter is anything that has mass and takes up space. • Volume is the measure of the amount of space occupied by matter.	• Make observations. • Collect, classify, and analyze data. • Create data tables. • Draw inferences. • Communicate findings.	• Change is everywhere. • Change can be natural or manmade.
12	Evaporation Findings	To understand evaporation and draw conclusions about findings from the principal's ocean water experiment. To continue work on an independent investigation.	• Matter is anything that has mass and takes up space. • Matter can change from one state to another; these changes are referred to as physical changes. • Temperature and energy can create physical changes in matter. • Materials are composed of parts that are too small to see without magnification.	• Create meaning from the experiment. • Tell others what was found.	• Change is everywhere. • Change is linked to time. • Change can be random or predictable. • Change can be natural or manmade.
13	Condensation	To investigate condensation by examining ice in a bag. To continue work on an independent investigation.	• Matter is anything that has mass and takes up space. • Matter can change from one state to another; these changes are referred to as physical changes. • Temperature and energy can create physical changes in matter. • Materials are composed of parts that are too small to see without magnification.	• Make observations. • Ask questions. • Design an experiment. • Create meaning from the experiment.	• Change is everywhere. • Change is linked to time.
14	Planning the Investigation and Hosting the Matter Conference	To practice and prepare for the matter conference.	• All common substances are made of matter. • Matter is anything that has mass and takes up space. • There are three states of matter: solids, liquids, and gases. • Objects can be described by color, shape, texture, relative size and weight, and position. • Matter can change from one state to another; these changes are referred to as physical changes. • Volume is the measure of the amount of space occupied by matter. • Mass is measure of the amount of matter. • Physical properties remain the same when a material is reduced in size. • Some liquids separate when mixed with water. • Some solids will dissolve in water, and more quickly in hot than cold water. • Temperature and energy can create physical changes in matter. • Materials are composed of parts that are too small to see without magnification.	• Make observations. • Ask questions. • Learn more about observations and questions. • Design and conduct experiments. • Create meaning from the experiment. • Tell others what was found.	• Change is everywhere. • Change is related to time. • Change can be natural or manmade. • Change can be random or predictable.

Lesson #	Title	Instructional Purpose	Essential Science Understandings	Scientific Investigation Skills and Processes	Change Generalizations
15	Concluding the Unit	To review the independent investigations from the matter conference. To review the science, process, and change concepts.	• All common substances are made of matter. • Matter is anything that has mass and takes up space. • There are three states of matter: solids, liquids, and gases. • Objects can be described by color, shape, texture, relative size and weight, and position. • Matter can change from one state to another; these changes are referred to as physical changes. • Volume is the measure of the amount of space occupied by matter. • Mass is measure of the amount of matter. • Physical properties remain the same when a material is reduced in size. • Some liquids separate when mixed with water. • Some solids will dissolve in water, and more quickly in hot than cold water. • Temperature and energy can create physical changes in matter. • Materials are composed of parts that are too small to see without magnification.	• Make observations. • Ask questions. • Learn more about observations and questions. • Design and conduct experiments. • Create meaning from the experiment. • Tell others what was found.	• Change is everywhere. • Change is related to time. • Change can be natural or manmade. • Change can be random or predictable.
	Postassessments				

Preteaching Lesson: Science Safety

Planning the Preteaching

Instructional Purposes: To instill in students the importance of safety in the classroom; to outline science safety rules to be implemented throughout the unit.

Instructional Time: 45 minutes

Materials/Resources/Equipment:
- Plastic disposable gloves
- Safety goggles
- Chart paper
- Markers
- Transparencies of the Science Safety Guidelines (p. 25) and Science Safety Rules (p. 26)
- Sample materials, such as: a plant, a plastic bag of nonhazardous powdery substance (sugar works well), a closed jar of nonhazardous liquid (water), a lit candle, and a sharp object (knife)

Implementing the Lesson

Note: Please read the Science Safety Guidelines (p. 25) prior to teaching this lesson.

1. Display sample materials on a long table in front of students. Inform students that they will soon begin a science unit in which they will observe and study many different kinds of materials, such as these. Explain that it is important for students to practice safety during the investigations. Relate the necessity of science safety rules with those that already have been established in the classroom.
2. Display and define each item. Tell students that as a class they will create a list of rules they should follow when handling these materials. Have students think of how they can keep their bodies safe. Record these on chart paper.
3. Next, unveil the Science Safety Rules (p. 26) on an overhead or written out on chart paper. Have students compare the two lists. How do students' examples relate to these rules? If necessary, add additional rules to the list.
4. Explain why some materials (such as knives) or elements (such as fire) are never appropriate for children to handle in school. Briefly discuss the potential hazards associated with these.
5. Finally, conduct a brief demonstration to illustrate how to practice safety guidelines. Take the plastic bag containing a nonhazardous powdery substance and the jar of nonhazardous liquid. Explain that you are going to investigate how the two materials interact. Ask students how you can be safe while doing this investigation. Reinforce that substances can be harmful to the eyes or skin and that they never should be ingested. Explain that the same is true of plants, which can be toxic to humans. Emphasize that students should follow similar guidelines when studying plants.
6. Following students' examples of safety measures, demonstrate how to use safety goggles to protect the eyes, plastic gloves to protect the hands, and other relevant

protective measures, such as pinning long hair back and wearing appropriate clothing. Conduct the demonstration by carefully pouring the powdery substance into the jar of liquid. Emphasize that you should never touch your face or mouth (and especially should not eat or drink) during science experiments.

7. Tell students that the teacher will dispose of materials properly after the investigation is completed. Students should not touch any potentially harmful substances.

8. Demonstrate the final rule, wash your hands, by properly removing the gloves (without the outside of the gloves ever touching the body) and the goggles. If there is a sink in the classroom, demonstrate how to properly wash one's hands. If no sink is present, inform students that after each investigation the class will go to the bathroom to wash their hands.

9. Conclude the lesson by emphasizing that science investigations are interesting and fun, but they also can be dangerous if not conducted properly. By following the Science Safety Rules, the class will enjoy the benefits of learning about science.

Science Safety Guidelines

1. Know and follow your school's policies and procedures regarding classroom safety.

2. Always provide direct adult supervision when students are engaging in scientific experimentation.

3. Ensure that all materials and equipment are safe for handling by primary students.

4. Exert extra caution when materials have the potential for harm when used improperly.

5. Use protective gear for eyes, skin, and breathing when conducting experiments and require students to do the same.

6. Always conduct an experiment by yourself before completing it with the students.

7. Store materials for experiments out of the reach of students.

8. Never allow students to eat or drink during science experiments.

9. Follow general safety rules for sharp objects, heated items, breakables, or spilled liquids.

10. Teach students that it is unsafe to touch their face, mouth, eyes, or other body parts when they are working with plants, animals, microorganisms, or chemicals. Wash hands prior to touching. Caution students about putting anything in their mouth or breathing in the smell of substances.

11. Be aware of students' allergies to plants, including plant pollen, animals, foods, chemicals, or other substances to be used in the science classroom. Take all precautions necessary. Common food allergens include peanuts, tree nuts (cashews, almonds, walnuts, hazelnuts, macadamia nuts, pecans, pistachios, and pine nuts), shellfish, fish, milk, eggs, wheat, and soy.

12. Use caution with plants. Never allow students to pick or handle any unknown plants, leaves, flowers, seeds, or berries. Use gloves to touch unknown plants. Many common house, garden, and wooded area plants are toxic.

13. Avoid glass jars and containers. Use plastic, paper, or cloth containers.

14. Thermometers should be filled with alcohol, not mercury.

15. Clearly label any chemicals used and dispose of properly.

Science Safety Rules

1. **Always** do scientific experiments with an adult person present.

2. **Never** mix things together (liquids, powders) without adult approval.

3. **Use** your senses carefully. Protect your eyes, ears, nose, mouth, and skin.

4. **Wash your hands** after using materials for an experiment.

Preassessment

Planning the Preassessment

Instructional Purpose: To determine prior knowledge of unit content.

Instructional Time:
- Concept assessment: 30 minutes
- Scientific process assessment: 20 minutes
- Content assessment: 30 minutes

Materials/Resources/Equipment Needed:
- Copies of preassessments for unit concept, process, and content
- Pencils

Implementing the Lesson

1. Explain to students that the class is beginning a new unit of study. Tell them that they will be completing a preassessment to determine what they already know about the topic. Assure them that the assessment is not for a grade and encourage them to do their best.
2. Collect the preassessments and debrief with students to begin building their understanding of the unit concept, process, and content. Briefly review each assessment and discuss some of the responses in general, indicating that this unit will provide them with more knowledge and skills than they now have.
3. Score the preassessments, using the rubrics provided. Keep the scores for diagnostic purposes in organizing grouping and various activities during the unit.

Name:_____ Date:_____

Preassessment for Change Concept

1. Give as many examples of things that change as you can, up to 10.

- _____
- _____
- _____
- _____
- _____
- _____
- _____
- _____
- _____
- _____

2. Draw one example of something that changes, showing before and after the change. Provide as many details as you can.

Before

After

Name:_____ Date:_____

3. Identify five ways that a tree could change or be changed.

- _____

- _____

- _____

- _____

- _____

4. What are *three* things you can say about all change?

All change

_____

_____

_____

All change

_____

_____

_____

All change

_____

_____

_____

Preassessment for Change Concept:
Grading Rubric

		5	4	3	2	1	0
1	**Examples of the Concept**	At least 9–10 appropriate examples are given.	At least 7–8 appropriate examples are given.	At least 5–6 appropriate examples are given.	At least 3 appropriate examples are given.	At least 1–2 appropriate examples are given.	No examples are given.
2	**Drawing of Before–After**	The drawing contains at least five changed elements depicting a before–after situation.	The drawing contains four changed elements depicting a before–after situation.	The drawing contains three changed elements that depict a before–after situation.	The drawing contains two elements and does not clearly indicate a change relationship.	The drawing contains only one picture element or does not show a before–after relationship.	The drawing contains no elements.
3	**Types of Change**	Five different types of changes are identified.	Four different types of changes are identified.	Three different types of changes are identified.	Two different types of changes are identified.	One different type of change is identified.	No type of change is identified.
4	**Generalizations**	Reflects three appropriate generalizations about change.	Reflects three somewhat appropriate generalizations about change.	Reflects two appropriate generalizations about change.	Reflects one appropriate generalization about change.	Reflects only a statement about change.	No statements or generalizations about change are provided.

Total Points: _____ / 20

Name:_____ Date:_____

Preassessment for Scientific Process

1. How would you study the following question: Are plants attracted to the sun?

_____

_____

_____

_____

_____

2. Describe an experiment to test this question that includes the following:

   a. Make a prediction regarding the question: Are plants attracted to the sun?

   I predict that

   _____

   _____

   _____

   _____

   _____

   b. What materials will be needed to conduct the experiment?

   _____

   _____

   _____

   _____

   _____

   _____

c. What steps must be taken to conduct the experiment and in what order?

_____

_____

_____

_____

_____

d. What data do you want to collect and how should it be recorded?

_____

_____

_____

_____

e. How do the data help me decide if my prediction is correct? Explain.

_____

_____

_____

_____

Name:_____ Date:_____

Preassessment for Scientific Process: Grading Rubric

	Criteria	Strong Evidence 3	Some Evidence 2	Little Evidence 1	No Evidence 0
2a.	**Generates a prediction.**	Clearly generates a prediction appropriate to the experiment.	Somewhat generates a prediction appropriate to the experiment.	Generates an inappropriate prediction.	Fails to generate a prediction.
2b.	**Lists materials needed.**	Provides an inclusive and appropriate list of materials. Provides a list of 5–6 materials.	Provides a partial list of appropriate materials needed. Provides a list of 3–4 materials.	Provides inappropriate materials. OR Provides only 1–2 appropriate materials.	Fails to provide a list of materials needed.
2c.	**Lists experiment steps.**	Clearly and concisely lists 4 or more steps as appropriate for the experiment design.	Clearly and concisely lists 2–3 steps as appropriate for the experiment design.	Generates at least 1 appropriate step.	Fails to generate experiment steps.
2c.	**Arranges steps in sequential order.**	N/A	Lists experiment steps in sequential order.	Lists 2 or fewer experiment steps or places them in an illogical order.	Does not list steps.
2d.	**Plans data collection.**	Clearly states a plan for data collection, including what data will be needed and how they will be recorded.	States a partial plan for data collection, citing some items for collection and some way of recording data.	Provides an incomplete plan for either data collection or recording.	Fails to identify any part of a plan for data collection.
2e.	**States plan for interpreting data for making predictions.**	Clearly states plan for interpreting data by linking data to prediction.	States a partial plan for interpreting data that links data to prediction.	Provides a brief statement that partially addresses use of data for prediction.	Fails to state plan for using data for making a prediction.

Total Score: _____ / 17

Note. Adapted from Fowler, M. (1990). The diet cola test. *Science Scope, 13,* 32–34.

Preassessment for Content: Teacher Directions

Explain to students that sometimes we know a lot about something even before our teachers teach it in school. Sometimes we don't know very much at all, but we like to learn new things.

For example, ask students, "What would you think about if someone asked you to tell all you know about how *farms* work? What are some of the words you would use?" List these on a chart. Then ask, "What are some of the things that happen on a farm?" List these on your chart as well. Then say, "I am going to show you a way I might tell about everything I know about how farms work." Begin a concept map on a large sheet of paper, using pictures and words, making simple links and emphasizing these links. Ask students to make their own maps on their drawing paper. This practice activity can be done with a partner. Share some of the resulting concept maps, encouraging students to articulate their links.

Read the following paragraph to students.

Today I would like you to think about all of the things you know about matter. Think about the words you would use and the pictures you could draw to make a concept map. Think about the connections you can make. On your concept map paper, draw in pictures and words that you know about matter. You will be drawing a concept map, just like the ones you did when we discussed the farm. The subject of your concept map is: "Tell me everything you know about matter."

Have students draw a second concept map on their own paper, this time making the focus of the map "matter."

Name:_____ Date:_____

Preassessment for Content: Grading Rubric

		5	4	3	2	1	0
1	**Hierarchical Level** *Each subordinate concept is more specific and less general than the concept drawn above it. Count the number of levels included in the total map.*	Five or more levels are identified.	Four levels are identified.	Three levels are identified	Two levels are identified.	One level is identified.	No hierarchical levels are identified.
2	**Propositions** *The linking of two concepts indicating a clear relationship is given. Count the total number of propositions identified on the total map.*	Student provides more than 12 propositions.	Student provides 10–12 propositions.	Student provides 7–9 propositions.	Student provides 4–6 propositions.	Student provides 1–3 propositions.	Student provides no propositions.
3	**Examples** *A valid example of a concept is provided. Count the total number of examples.*	Student provides more than 12 examples.	Student provides 10–12 examples.	Student provides 7–9 examples.	Student provides 4–6 examples.	Student provides 1–3 examples.	Student provides no examples.

Total Points: _____ / 15

Lesson 1:
What Is Change?

Planning the Lesson

Instructional Purpose: To understand the concept of change and apply change generalizations.

Instructional Time: 45 minutes

Essential Science Understandings: Some liquids separate when mixed with water.

Change Concept Generalizations:
- Change is everywhere.
- Change is related to time.
- Change can be natural or manmade.
- Change can be random or predictable.

What to Look for in Assessment:
- Can students brainstorm things that change and classify them into categories?
- Can students provide examples of each of the change generalizations?
- Can students apply the change generalizations to the water, oil, and ice experiment?

Materials/Resources/Equipment:
- One pack of sticky notes per group of 3–4 students
- Chart paper for each group of 3–4 with Taba Concept Model Chart for students to complete
- Markers
- Four sentence strips with a different change generalization written on each strip
- Ice cubes (made with water mixed with a couple drops of blue food coloring)
- Vegetable oil
- Water in clear jar, half full
- Student lab books, one for each student

> **Teacher's Note:** Prior to the lesson, fill an ice cube tray with water and add blue food coloring to the ice cubes. You'll need a colored ice cube, oil, and water for this lesson.

Implementing the Lesson

1. Tell students they are going to begin thinking like a scientist and studying change. Tell them that scientists study change using their senses. Ask students to give examples of changes scientists might study using each sense.
2. In front of the class, fill a clear jar halfway full with water. Pour vegetable oil in the glass, about an inch from the rim, and mix. Allow students to watch as the oil and water separate. Ask students to observe what happened with their senses. Which senses did they use? What did they discover about oil and water? Discuss changes that happened. Next, drop a colored ice cube in the oil so that it is suspended. Tell students that you are going to leave the ice cube in the oil and from time to time

36

throughout the lesson you are going to study changes that happen to the water, oil, and ice cube, but first you need to learn more about the concept of change.

3. Display the Taba Concept Model Chart on chart paper. It should look similar to this, with enough room for students to write:

Taba Concept Model Chart

Examples of Change	Categories of Change
Nonexamples of Change	Generalizations About Change

4. Create small groups of 3–4 students. Give each group sticky notes, markers, and a chart with the above Taba concept graphic. Ask each group to brainstorm examples of anything it can think of that changes and write or draw one idea per sticky note. Circulate as the groups complete this task to make sure that the students understand the task. Have each group share its examples with the whole class and write examples from each group on the whole class chart. After the groups have shared, they will need to place their sticky notes on their group chart section labeled "Examples of Change."

5. Talk about what it means to classify things, modeling the classification of objects into different categories and referring to several ideas of possible categories. Remind students that in order to classify objects, they must find some way in which the objects are *similar* or alike. Ask groups to classify their sticky notes of change examples into categories. Once the students are satisfied with their categories, they will group them together in the "Categories of Change" box of their chart. Then, they will label each category. Each group will share its categories with the whole class and the teacher will write down the categories on the section of the class chart labeled "Categories of Change."

6. In their groups, have students brainstorm nonexamples of change. Again, the student will write one example per sticky note and each group will share its nonexamples with the whole class, as the teacher writes the nonexamples on the section of the class chart labeled "Nonexamples of Change."

7. Ask the students what they know about change by looking at the examples and nonexamples. Provide the students one example as a model (e.g., "I notice that there are many different kinds of changes.") Write down your statement on the section of the class chart labeled "Generalizations About Change." Explain that scientists often *generalize* or make statements about what they notice across

several examples, observations, or investigations, and these generalizations help scientists to understand our world. In order to make generalizations, scientists must infer how the examples, observations, or investigations are alike.

8. Ask the students to pretend that they are scientists and have each group come up with one generalization about change. Ask them to write that example on the chart statement labeled "Generalizations About Change." Circulate as the students work in small groups to facilitate understanding of the generalization. Ask groups to share their generalizations.

9. Present the following generalizations by pasting prewritten sentence strips with generalizations in the section of the class chart labeled "Generalizations About Change" and explain that the students will be looking at how these generalizations help scientists to understand matter:
   a. Change is everywhere.
   b. Change is related to time.
   c. Change can be natural or manmade.
   d. Change may be random or predictable.

10. Post the completed chart in the classroom and tell students you will be discussing changes in their world throughout the next few weeks.

11. Refer students back to the oil, water, and ice cube. They should note that the ice cube is melting and as the ice melts, it turns into a liquid and goes to the bottom of the glass because oil and water don't mix. Explain to the students that during this unit they will be studying different changes that happen in our world including changes in matter. Tell them they will learn more about matter later, but matter is anything that has mass and takes up space. Matter is all around us—everything that we see, feel, and/or touch is made of matter.

12. Ask students to look at the change generalizations you just discussed and determine which ones scientists might use to describe the oil, water, and ice cube changes. Have students defend their answers. Make sure students explain changes that happened in the experiment using the change generalizations. Questions might include:
   a. How did the experiment show changes over time?
   b. Do you think the changes in the ice cube melting are random or predictable? Why?
   c. What are some of the natural changes that occurred in the experiment? Manmade changes?

13. Concluding Questions/Actions:
   a. How do you think scientists study change?
   b. Why is the concept of change useful when observing the ice, oil, and water?
   c. How might our senses help us investigate change? Are there other ways to investigate changes in our world?
   d. What does a scientist have to do in order to make a generalization?
   e. Do you think that a generalization is always true? Why or why not?

14. Distribute one lab book to each student. Explain that scientists keep a log of their investigations and they date each entry put in their log. Tell students they will be keeping a log of their investigations each day. Ask them to date their first page and respond to the following prompt:
   a. Change is important in science because . . .
   b. Ask students to share responses, as time allows.

Extending the Lesson

What to Do at Home

- Talk with a family member about a time in which a change had a positive effect on the family. Be prepared to share your example with the class.

Lesson 2:
What Is a Scientist?

Planning the Lesson

Instructional Purposes: To analyze characteristics of scientists; to learn about investigation skills that scientists use.

Instructional Time: 45 minutes

Essential Science Understanding: This lesson focuses on scientific investigation processes.

Scientific Investigation Skills and Processes:
- Make observations.
- Ask questions.
- Learn more.
- Design and conduct experiments.
- Create meaning.
- Tell others what was found.

What to Look for in Assessment:
- Can students distinguish between scientists and nonscientists?
- Can students identify scientific investigation processes used by scientists?

Materials/Resources/Equipment:
- Lab coat (can be a white T-shirt or undershirt)
- Beaker
- Microscope
- Prepared charts or transparencies of Frayer Model of Vocabulary Development on Scientists and Incomplete Frayer Model of Vocabulary Development on Scientists (pp. 43–44)
- One chart of Incomplete Frayer Model of Vocabulary Development on Scientists for each group of 3–4 students
- *What Is a Scientist?* by Barbara Lehn
- Markers or pens
- Nametags
- Word wall cards: scientist, observation, prediction, hypothesis, investigation, experiment
- Student lab books

Implementing the Lesson

1. Put on a lab coat and pick up a beaker and microscope. Ask the students what kind of job you might have. Explain that you are a *scientist*. Ask the students if they know a scientist and

> **Teacher's Note:** This lesson can be skipped if students have had the lesson previously.

allow them to discuss what they know about scientists or their experiences with scientists.

2. Display the completed Frayer Model of Vocabulary Development on Scientists (p. 43). Cover entries in each section with sticky notes so students cannot read them until the appropriate time. Ask the students to define a scientist. Write down their definition on the board.

3. Uncover the definition section of the Frayer graphic to reveal the following definition of a scientist: "a person who studies nature and the physical world by testing, experimenting, and measuring" (Scholastic, 1996) and ask the class to compare and contrast the official definition with the class' definition.

4. Divide class into small groups of 3–4 students. Explain and assign roles to each student in the group: recorder, reporter, supporter (manages materials, keeps the group on task, and encourages the group), and timekeeper.

5. Give each group the Incomplete Frayer Model of Vocabulary Development on Scientist (p. 44) on chart paper with the definition in the appropriate section. Ask groups to write down what a scientist does in the appropriate section (scientific investigation processes). Have reporters share group answers with the class.

6. Uncover the section titled "What Scientists Do . . ." to show the science process skills. Allow students to compare and contrast what they wrote down earlier with the list below. Explain the skills and tell students that they will learn more about the science process later in this unit. The skills are:
    a. Make observations.
    b. Ask questions.
    c. Learn more.
    d. Design and conduct experiments.
    e. Create meaning.
    f. Tell others what was found.

7. Explain that there are many different types of scientists; for example, a meteorologist is someone who studies the weather, which includes temperature, wind, precipitation, and air pressure, and how these factors relate to each other. Have groups write down different types of scientists. Share responses with the class and then compare and contrast with the types listed on the large group chart. Note that most of the words end with the suffix "ist" and that this suffix means "a person who."

8. Repeat the last process, asking the students to give nonexamples of scientists, and then share responses. Lead students in a discussion using these questions:
    a. Explain whether you think everyone can be a scientist.
    b. What makes a scientist a scientist?
    c. When is someone not a scientist?

9. Explain that the students are going to learn how to become scientists by learning how to think like a scientist and learning about what scientists do. Read aloud the book *What Is a Scientist?* Prior to reading, tell students to look for the scientific investigation processes. Refer to the "What Scientists Do . . ." list. After reading the book, discuss the following questions with students:
    a. What scientific investigation skills did we read about in the book?
    b. What scientific investigation processes do you use? When do you use them?
    c. What is something that you would like to investigate?

10. Have students put on lab coats (these can be white T-shirts or undershirts) and nametags reading "Professor (child's name)."
11. Distribute lab books to each student. Remind students to put a date on the next blank page and respond to the prompt, "To think like a scientist means I will . . ." Have students share their responses if time allows.
12. Concluding Questions/Actions:
    a. Describe how scientists study change.
    b. Describe whether or not you would like to be a scientist and why.

Extending the Lesson

What to Do at Home
- Ask students to ask their parent or some other adult to respond to one of the following questions: "What would you do to think like a scientist?" or "What would you investigate if you were a scientist and how would you investigate it?"

Frayer Model of Vocabulary Development on Scientists

Definition "…a person who studies nature and the physical world by testing, experimenting, and measuring"	**What Scientists Do . . .** **(Scientific Investigation Processes)** • Make observations. • Ask questions. • Learn more. • Design and conduct experiments. • Create meaning. • Tell others what was found.
Examples • Astronomers—study the universe (planets, stars, etc.) • Biologists—study life (plants and animals) • Geologists—study the earth's layers of soil and rocks • Physicists—study matter and energy	**Nonexamples** • An entertainer • A poet • A banker

Scientists

Incomplete Frayer Model of Vocabulary Development on Scientists

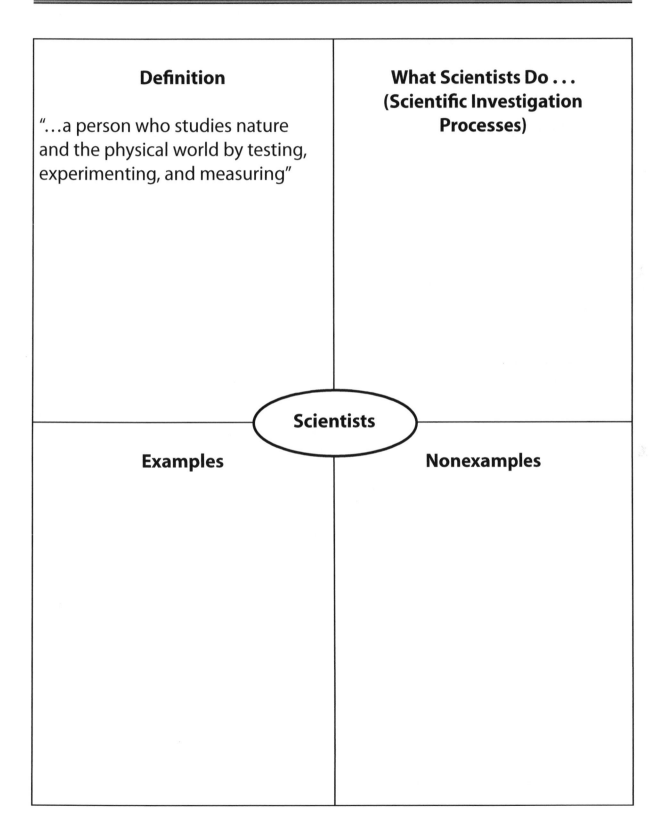

Definition

"…a person who studies nature and the physical world by testing, experimenting, and measuring"

What Scientists Do . . . (Scientific Investigation Processes)

Scientists

Examples

Nonexamples

Lesson 3:
Introduction to Matter

Planning the Lesson

Instructional Purposes: To identify, observe, and investigate the properties of the three states of matter.

Instructional Time: 30–45 minutes

Essential Science Understandings:
- All common substances are made of matter.
- Matter is anything that has mass and takes up space.
- There are three states of matter: solids, liquids, and gases.
- Objects can be described by color, shape, texture, relative size and weight, and position.

Scientific Investigation Skills and Processes:
- Make observations.
- Collect, classify, and analyze data.
- Communicate findings.

What to Look for in Assessment:
- Can students work together cooperatively during the activity?
- Can students record their observations and conclusions correctly?
- Can students correctly apply the steps of the investigation process?
- Can students use new vocabulary in group discussion (e.g., solid, liquid, gas; definitions of solid, liquid, and gas)?
- Can students specifically articulate the properties of a solid, liquid, and gas?
- Can students generate examples fairly easily?

Materials/Resources/Equipment:
- Gather several materials from the classroom or home for groups of 4–5 students. Include examples of solids, liquids, and gases. Ideas might be stuffed animals, textbooks, wooden blocks, shaving cream, bottle of soda, maple syrup, blown-up balloon, bottle of water, food coloring, empty see-through plastic bowls with lids, and so forth.
- Clear plastic container filled with water
- Glass
- Paper towel
- Plastic eggs that separate into two pieces (three eggs per group)
- Play dough and/or blocks for eggs
- Water and/or syrup for eggs
- 2-liter bottle, emptied
- Balloon
- Something sharp to poke a hole in a 2-liter bottle (keep safety in mind)
- Word wall cards: matter, states, properties, solid, liquid, gas
- Copies of Properties of Matter handout (p. 50)

- Transparency or copies of Introduction to Matter Concept Map (p. 51)
- Student lab books

Implementing the Lesson

1. Review with students what a scientist is and what scientists do. Tell students they are going to act like a scientist today by using the skills of observing, classifying, and analyzing.
2. Divide students into groups. Give each group a set of materials. Materials do not have to be the same but should include examples of liquids, solids, and gases.
3. Ask students to categorize their examples using their five senses or other methods they may come up with.
4. After students have had time to categorize, ask them to share how they made their categories.
5. Put a T-chart on the board with one column labeled "Made of Matter" and the other column labeled "Not Made of Matter." Explain to students that they are working with matter.
6. Write the following definition of matter on the board: "Matter is anything that has mass and takes up space."

> **Teacher's Note:** This lesson requires preparation prior to teaching the lesson. Fill enough separate eggs for one per group of each of the following:
>
> Egg 1: Play dough or a block
> Egg 2: Water or maple syrup
> Egg 3: Nothing (just air)
>
> To differentiate the lesson you may give different groups eggs filled with solids or liquids. For example, play dough and maple syrup may be more difficult to decipher as a solid or liquid than water and a block. If Internet access is available, show students "What are the three states of matter?" from NASA's KSNN Web page at http://ksnn.larc.nasa.gov/k2/s_statesMatter_v.html

7. Tell students that everything on earth that we see, touch, or smell is made up of matter. You are made up of matter. The chair you are sitting on is made up of matter. So are the walls and floor, the books in class, the sandwich you eat for lunch, and the air you breathe. Ask students to name some other things in the classroom that are made up of matter. Write the list in the first column of the T-chart.
8. Now ask students to name some things that are not made up of matter and write those on the board in the second column. Thoughts are one example, as are dreams. A poem is not made up of matter, but the page it is written on is.
9. Explain to students that scientists have classified materials or matter into three different forms, called *states*. These states are solid, liquid, and gas. Introduce students to the idea that plasma now is considered a fourth state of matter. Plasma exists at very high temperatures and molecules in that state can behave very differently. Plasma does not naturally occur on earth because of the very high temperatures that are required, and therefore, you should know about it, but we will only focus on the three main states of matter. Draw a chart on the board with three categories, labeled with Solids, Liquids, and Gases. Provide at least one example of each type of matter.
10. Ask students to revisit the materials in their group and see if they can place their matter into three categories (solids, liquids, and gases) that emphasize the states of matter. Remind them to also consider what is *inside* a container, as well as the container itself.

11. Once students have had time to re-sort their categories, ask them to figure out what each category has in common. In other words, how would they define a solid, a liquid, and a gas? What properties or characteristics does each have in common?

12. While students are discussing common characteristics, distribute the Properties of Matter handout (p. 50). Draw a similar table on the board.

13. Ask students what properties each category has in common. Brainstorm a list of properties for each category. Students may have a difficult time coming up with gases. Explain to them that gases include the air we breathe, bubbles in soda, or air in a balloon, for example. Emphasize that an empty container is a solid, but that it is filled with a gas (air). Use a balloon as another example. The balloon is a solid, but it is filled with a gas.

14. Ask students what characteristics they noticed about each of their categories. Help them come to the conclusion that:
    a. A gas moves and fills up the container it is in.
    b. A liquid takes the shape of its container.
    c. A solid has a shape you can see (and usually feel).

    Help students finish completing the Properties of Matter handout by copying the above conclusions under each category and writing an example.

15. Ask students this question: "If we can't see gas, how do we know that it's there?" Conduct the following model activities to demonstrate the presence of air in a bottle.
    a. Show an "empty" glass. Shake the glass. Select students to put their ear to the glass. Ask students what they see and hear. Wad a dry paper towel and place it into the bottom of the glass so that it stays in the glass when you turn it upside down. Take a plastic tub and fill it with water. Ask students what will happen to the paper towel if you place the glass upside down in the water. Allow time for predictions. Plunge the glass with the paper towel into the water so that the bottom of the glass rests on the bottom of the container filled with water. Carefully remove the glass and the dry paper towel. Why is the paper towel still dry? Why didn't water go in to the glass? Explain to students that the air trapped the paper towel in the glass and would not let water in. Therefore, there was air in the glass even though you couldn't see it.
    b. Next, take an ordinary balloon and blow it up in front of the class. Deflate it. Hook the mouth of the same balloon over the outside of a 2-liter bottle and then push the balloon to the inside of the bottle. Challenge someone in the class to blow up the balloon inside the bottle. This cannot be done. Ask students why the balloon couldn't be blown up. They should conclude that air inside the bottle is taking up space and won't allow the balloon to inflate. Next, poke a small hole in the bottom or side of the 2-liter bottle. Now ask someone to blow up the balloon. The balloon should inflate because the gases in the air can spread out and escape into the room, allowing room for the balloon to inflate.

16. Provide each student or group of students with three plastic eggs: one with a block or play dough, one with water or maple syrup, and one with air. Tell students you found these mystery eggs and you need to determine what is inside of them without opening them. Ask them to continue to use their scientific skills and what they've just learned about matter to determine what type of matter might be inside each egg.

17. Ask students how they might determine what type of matter is inside each egg. (Answers may include shaking the eggs, listening to the sounds, rolling the eggs,

smelling the eggs, and so forth.) Allow time for the students to play with the eggs to determine what type of matter is inside.

18. Instruct students that they may now open their eggs to confirm their predictions. Note: You may want students to open eggs over a sink or empty container. Ask students if their predictions were accurate.

19. The next part of this lesson involves concept mapping. Please see the Concept Mapping Section in Appendix A as a guide for instructing students in concept mapping. To begin this activity, tell students: "We have just begun studying about matter. Let's review what we have learned. I am going to teach you how you can show what you have learned in a way that will help you remember." Distribute copies or show students the transparency of Introduction to Matter Concept Map (p. 51). Tell students: "We have learned two things about matter so far." Use the following questions as a guide for completing the concept map activity. See Figure 3 below for guidance.
    a. What does all matter have?
    b. What does matter take up?

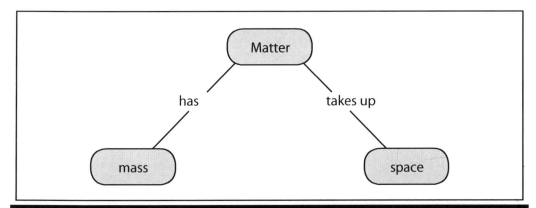

Figure 3. Example of concept mapping for matter.

20. Place the following words—states of matter, matter, properties, solids, liquids, and gases—on the word wall and tell students that as scientists, they should begin using those words when discussing their observations.

21. Concluding Questions/Actions:
    a. How did what you learned about the properties of matter help you decide what was in each egg before opening it?
    b. How did you discover what kind of matter was in each egg?
    c. How did this activity help you think more like a scientist? What skills did you use?
    d. What questions do you still have?

22. Ask students to respond to the following journal prompt in their lab books:
    a. What did you learn about matter today?

Extending the Lesson

Technology Connection
- NASA's KSNN (Kid's Science News Network) has 30-second "fastbreak" cartoon summaries of science concepts geared for students in grades K–2. It provides reinforcement for the concepts and can be used with the whole class or

bookmarked for a technology learning center. Visit http://ksnn.larc.nasa.gov/ k2/s_statesMatter_v.html.

- Harcourt Publishers has a "States of Matter" demonstration that offers a peek inside each state and reveals the differences at a molecular level. Visit http:// www.harcourtschool.com/activity/states_of_matter/.

What to Do at Home

- Play "I Spy Matter" with an adult or a sibling. Walk around the house and/or the yard finding different examples of solids, liquids, and gases. Say, "I spy a (solid, liquid, gas) that is (color, texture, size, shape, temperature)" and have the other person guess what you have "spied."

Name:_____ Date:_____

Properties of Matter

Directions: Write down your observations of each from your categories of items.

Solids	Liquids	Gases
Descriptions:	Descriptions:	Descriptions:
Properties:	Properties:	Properties:
Examples:	Examples:	Examples:

Name:_____ Date:_____

Introduction to Matter Concept Map

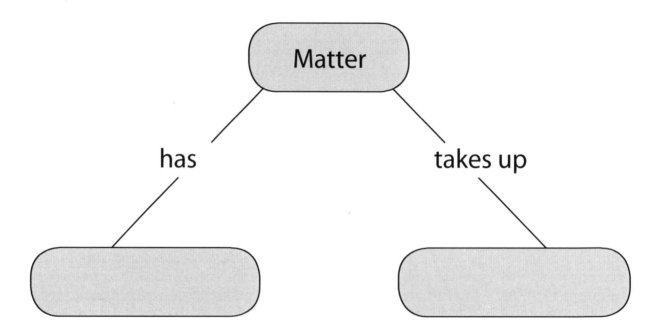

51

Lesson 4:
What Scientists Do:
Observe, Question, Learn More

Planning the Lesson

Instructional Purposes: To apply the Wheel of Scientific Investigation and Reasoning (make observations, ask questions, and learn more); to begin to investigate if the properties of a solid or liquid remain the same after a size change.

Instructional Time: 45 minutes

Essential Science Understandings:
- Objects can be described by color, shape, texture, relative size, weight, and position.
- There are three main states of matter: solids, liquids, and gases.
- Matter has physical properties that remain the same when reduced in size.

Scientific Investigation Skills and Processes:
- Make observations.
- Ask questions.
- Learn more.

What to Look for in Assessment:
- Can students apply the steps of scientific investigation to an experiment?
- Can students interpret data from a data table?

Materials/Resources/Equipment:
- Lab coat for teacher
- Lab coats for students
- Charts or transparencies of the Wheel of Scientific Investigation and Reasoning and Physical Properties of Solids and Liquids handouts (pp. 55–56)
- Foil
- Ice cubes in a plastic bag
- Student handouts or charts (if using small groups) of pages 55–56
- An array of solids and liquids for small groups of students including but not limited to foil, plastic pieces, old overhead transparencies, tongue depressors, thin wire, paper, cardboard, balloons, syrup, water, Kool-Aid, soda, shaving cream, ice cubes in a plastic bag, and so forth
- Student lab books

Implementing the Lesson

1. Have students put on their lab coats. Explain to students that they are going to learn to think like a scientist and use scientific processes.
2. Review the states of matter and the properties of matter. Ask students how they have been practicing the skills of thinking like a scientist.

3. Review the six processes introduced in Lesson 2: (1) make observations, (2) ask questions, (3) learn more, (4) design and conduct experiments, (5) create meaning, and (6) tell others what was found. Remind students that scientists use these processes when learning about their world.

4. Distribute copies of the Wheel of Scientific Investigation and Reasoning (p. 55) to all students and quickly overview the six components. Ask students to point out the relationship between the scientific investigation processes discussed the day before and those components included on the wheel, such as the following:

   a. What do you notice about the Wheel of Scientific Investigation and Reasoning?
   b. What processes do you think that scientists use before they conduct an experiment?
   c. What do scientists do to conduct an experiment?
   d. What do scientists do after they conduct an experiment?
   e. Which part of an investigation do you think would be most difficult? Why?

Create groups of 3–4 and assign roles for each group member. Review role responsibilities: recorder, reporter, supporter (manages materials, keeps the group on task, and encourages group members), and timekeeper.

5. Direct students to the top of the Wheel of Scientific Investigation and Reasoning (titled "Make Observations"). Explain to students that you want them to use their observation skills to think like a scientist.

6. Point out the existing safety concerns while experimenting; this is why scientists wear goggles when doing experiments. Also, point out to students that some materials can be poisonous or harmful, so students should not taste or touch them unless they are given specific instructions. Explain to students that you know what the substance is so you are going to allow the students to use their senses to make observations. Pose the following questions to students to reincorporate safety concerns:

   a. When might it be harmful to use some senses during an investigation?
   b. How should you decide when it is not safe to use some senses during an investigation?
   c. What are some ways that you can protect your senses during an investigation?

7. Explain that sometimes scientists use charts to write down observations. Divide students into groups of 4–5 and provide them with an array of solids and liquids such as foil, plastic pieces, old overhead transparencies, tongue depressors, thin wire, paper, cardboard, balloons, syrup, water, Kool-Aid, soda, shaving cream, ice cubes in a plastic bag, and so forth. Ask students the following questions:

   a. When you make observations, you use your senses to learn. What sense do you use most to make observations?
   b. Do you think scientists always use their sense of taste and smell? When might that be dangerous? (*Note*: Determine whether or not you will allow students to taste the liquids.)

8. Have the students work in their small groups for about 10 minutes and use the chart on the Physical Properties of Solids and Liquids handout (pp. 56–57) to record group observations of the different materials using their senses and classification skills. Invite the reporters to share their findings. Record the findings on a class chart in the front of the room. Include the following questions in the class discussion:
   a. What do you notice about our observations?
   b. How did you know to classify the objects as solids or liquids? What special characteristics does each category have?
   c. Are there other ways besides using senses and classifying to collect data on the objects?

9. Direct students' attention to the second section on the wheel ("Ask Questions"). Model this section by writing down the following question on a sentence strip (do this ahead of time): Do the properties of a solid or liquid remain the same if we change the size?

10. Ask students to tell you other questions they have about their materials and write their questions on a large piece of chart paper. Guide the class to pick your question (or one similar to it) as the one question they want to answer.

11. Refer to the third step on the wheel ("Learn More"). Ask students what can be done to learn more about something (i.e., Internet, books, experts), and what they think is the best way to learn. Require students to explain their answers.

12. Point out to students that one way they can learn more is through additional observations. Hold up a bag with the ice cubes in it. Ask students the following questions:
   a. What differences do you observe? What might cause the differences?
   b. What type of matter are the ice cubes? The melted ice cubes? How are they the same? Different?
   c. What about the foil? What happens when the foil is smooth and flat? What about when the foil is wadded into a ball? What do you observe?

13. Tell students that they are going to complete the remaining steps on the Wheel of Scientific Investigation and Reasoning the next day.

14. Ask students to place their ingredients in a sack or plastic tub until the next lesson.

15. Concluding Questions/Actions:
   a. How were you like a scientist today?
   b. What do you think we will do tomorrow in order to conduct an experiment on our question?

16. Ask students to answer the following question as a new entry in their lab books:
   a. When observing the various materials, I found that the _____ (sense) gave me the most helpful information because . . .

Extending the Lesson

What to Do at Home
   • Explain to your parents what a scientist does.
   • Design a lab coat at home and talk to your family about ways you act like a scientist at home.

Name:_____ Date:_____

Wheel of Scientific Investigation and Reasoning

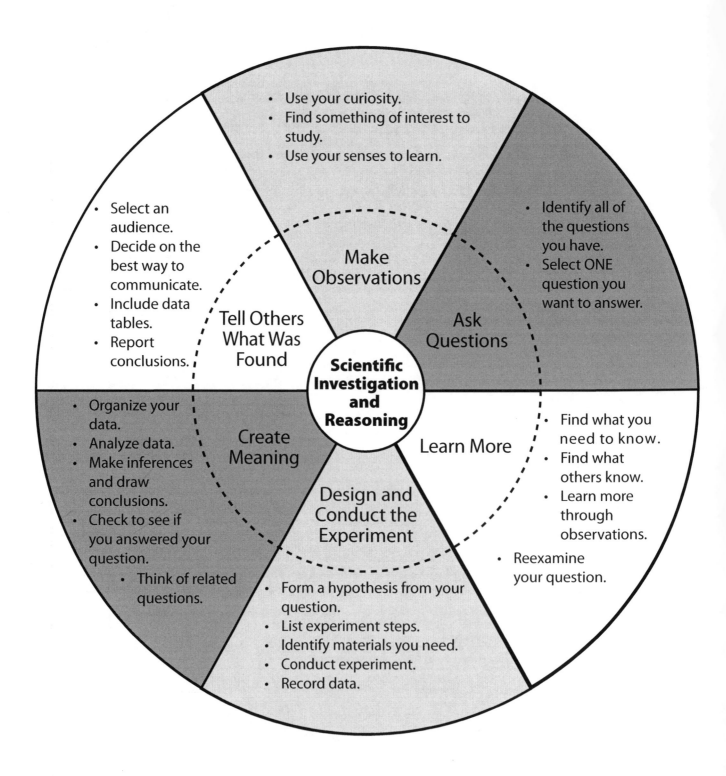

- Use your curiosity.
- Find something of interest to study.
- Use your senses to learn.

Make Observations

- Identify all of the questions you have.
- Select ONE question you want to answer.

Ask Questions

- Select an audience.
- Decide on the best way to communicate.
- Include data tables.
- Report conclusions.

Tell Others What Was Found

Scientific Investigation and Reasoning

Learn More

- Find what you need to know.
- Find what others know.
- Learn more through observations.
- Reexamine your question.

- Organize your data.
- Analyze data.
- Make inferences and draw conclusions.
- Check to see if you answered your question.
- Think of related questions.

Create Meaning

Design and Conduct the Experiment

- Form a hypothesis from your question.
- List experiment steps.
- Identify materials you need.
- Conduct experiment.
- Record data.

Name:_____ Date:_____

Physical Properties of Solids and Liquids

Record your observations and comparisons in the chart below.

Name of Material	Observations (Use your senses to describe how the material feels, looks, tastes [if safe], smells, and sounds)	Classification (Check one)	
		Solid	Liquid

Name:_____ Date:_____

In what ways are the materials the same?

_____

_____

_____

_____

_____

_____

_____

_____

In what ways are the materials different?

_____

_____

_____

_____

_____

_____

_____

_____

Lesson 5:
What Scientists Do: Experiment, Create Meaning, Tell Others

Planning the Lesson

Instructional Purposes: To design and conduct an experiment about what happens to the properties of matter when reduced in size; to create meaning from the experiment; to tell others what was found; to understand what the scenario is asking students to do.

Instructional Time: 45 minutes

Essential Science Understandings:
- Objects can be described by color shape, texture, relative size and weight, and position.
- Physical properties remain the same when a material changes in size.

Scientific Investigation Skills and Processes:
- Design and conduct experiments.
- Create meaning from the experiment.
- Tell others what was found.

Change Concept Generalizations:
- Change can be natural or manmade.
- Change can be random or predictable.

What to Look for in Assessment:
- Can students apply the steps of scientific investigation?
- Can students interpret data from a data table?
- Can students describe how the experiment was conducted and what results were found?
- Can students apply their knowledge of the properties of solids and liquids to the experiment?
- Can students record data appropriately?

Materials/Resources/Equipment:
- Lab coat for teacher
- Lab coats for students
- Prepared charts or transparencies of work done during the previous lesson
- Prepared charts or transparencies of the Wheel of Scientific Investigation and Reasoning (p. 55), Scientific Investigation Sheet (p. 62), Experiment Process (p. 63), Data Table: Part I (p. 64), and Data Table: Part II (p. 65)
- Student handouts of Wheel of Scientific Investigation and Reasoning (p. 55), Scientific Investigation Sheet (p. 62), Experiment Process (p. 63), Data Table: Part I (p. 64), Data Table: Part II (p. 65), and Superintendent's Letter (p. 66)

- One badge per student using page 67; can be printed on colored paper or labels
- Copy of the Superintendent's Letter in an envelope
- An array of solids such as: foil, scrap plastic bottles or old overhead transparencies, tongue depressors, thin wire, paper, cardboard, or a balloon
- An array of liquids such as: syrup, water, soda, molasses, or Kool-Aid
- Scissors
- Measuring spoons and cups
- Towels
- Empty containers for liquids
- Sticky notes
- Student lab books

Implement the Lesson

1. Review what the class did during the previous lessons. Remind students of the ice cube, oil, and water experiment from Lesson 1. Ask students what happened to the ice cube. What happened to the water from the melted ice cube? (Students should be able to articulate that the ice cube, even though it was melting, acted as a solid. Once the ice cube melted, it started acting like a liquid by sinking to the bottom of the oil and turning the water blue.) Ask students:
   a. What states of matter were examined using the ice cube, oil, and water experiment?
   b. What did we start investigating yesterday?
   c. How did we begin our investigation and what scientific processes did we apply?
   d. What did we observe about our different materials?

2. Ask students to vote as to whether they want to study liquids or solids. Divide students into smaller groups of 3–4 based on their choice of whether they chose liquids or solids.
3. Show students the Wheel of Scientific Investigation and Reasoning (p. 55). Explain what they did in parts 1–3. Move to the fourth process ("Design and Conduct the Experiment"). Note that the first thing scientists do to conduct an experiment is to form a hypothesis from their question. Write the following definition of the word *hypothesis* on the board and discuss its meaning with students: "a temporary prediction about how a scientific investigation or experiment will turn out that can be tested."
4. Have students either turn to their partner or talk in small groups about other possible hypotheses that could come from the question and write down the hypotheses on chart paper, asking the following questions of the student groups:
   a. What other hypotheses could we form from the original question?
   b. How did you come up with this hypothesis?

5. Distribute the Scientific Investigation Sheet (p. 62). Help students complete the sheet.
6. Explain that the hypothesis needs to be tested and to do that we do an experiment. It is important to plan the experiment by listing the steps. Ask students to tell what they think needs to be done to conduct an experiment for the hypothesis. After students share, reveal the list of steps the class is going to follow. Distribute the Experiment Process handout (p. 63).

7. Explain that scientists have to be careful about how they test a hypothesis or how they plan an experiment. They must think about all of the different things that could cause something to happen and then make sure that the experiment changes only one of those things; in other words, they must identify the variables. Tell students, "Let's consider our experiment. What things could happen that might cause problems?"

8. Distribute four of the materials from the previous lesson to each group, based on whether or not they are studying solids or liquids. Next, brainstorm the list of materials the class is going to need. Direct students to the bottom of the Scientific Investigation Sheet. Ask students to write in the four materials they are testing, as well as additional materials they need to reduce the size of their matter (i.e., scissors, smaller cups).

9. Explain that scientists conduct each experiment more than once to make sure that what occurred isn't just a coincidence. The class is going to repeat the experiment by comparing different group findings. Point out that each group is going to do the same thing with solids or liquids at the same time. Ask yourself the following to prepare:
    a. Does each group have the same items?
    b. Does each group have the same steps to follow?

10. Guide the groups, step-by-step to conduct the experiment at the same time.

11. Tell the students that scientists use charts to organize their data so they can figure out or analyze what the data show— to *create meaning* from the charts. Distribute Data Table: Part 1 and Data Table: Part 2 (pp. 64–65). Ask each group to make observations and to write down what they observed before and after their experiments.

12. Refer students to the conclusion section of their data (Data Table: Part II). Ask them to complete their findings by filling in the appropriate sections. Ask students to compare their findings. Did everyone find the same things? Why or why not?

13. Tell students that they have just conducted a scientific investigation or experiment. They tested their hypothesis and now they need to do the last two processes:
    a. Create meaning.
    b. Tell others what was found.

14. In order to create meaning, explain that the students must be able to explain their findings. Tell students that you want to know how well they are able to create meaning as scientists. Discuss the following questions:
    a. What might we infer about different states of matter when their size is changed? Did it matter whether the matter is solid or liquid? Why or why not?
    b. Ask students to recall the ice in oil experiment. How does this experiment relate to the ice and oil experiment? Did the physical properties of the ice stay the same even though it was reduced in size? What about the water when more was added?
    c. What questions do you still have as a result of your experiment?
    d. Do you think the changes you observed in matter are manmade or natural? Provide examples of times when matter might be reduced in size because of manmade changes and times when matter might be reduced in size as part of a natural change.
    e. Do you think your findings would be the same if you used different objects? Explain your answer.
    f. Are the changes in the properties of matter random changes or predictable changes? Explain your answer.

g. Do you think the properties of a gas remain the same when reduced in size? How might you find out?

15. Explain that now the class needs to tell others what was found. Ask student pairs or small groups to decide whom we should tell about our experiment findings and how we should communicate our findings. Allow students to share with the whole class and lead them to see that one way they could communicate the results is by sharing the experiment data chart. What is important about what we found? How could the information that we found be useful?

16. After students have discussed how to share findings, explain that scientists sometimes share their findings with each other through writing articles in journals or magazines and by presenting their findings at conferences. Take the Superintendent's Letter (p. 66) out of an envelope and explain that it is interesting that the students are just learning about presenting their findings because you have a request from the superintendent. Read the letter to the class. Solicit responses and assure them that you will help them plan a conference where they can share their findings.

17. Give each student a small sticky note. Tell them to place the sticky note about two thirds of the way back in their lab book as a marker. Explain that throughout the next few lessons they can create a list of ideas and questions on this marked page in their journal for the Matter Conference.

18. Proclaim that the students, or scientists, have just conducted a scientific investigation and give out badges saying, "I Conducted a Scientific Investigation— Ask Me About It" (see p. 67).

19. Concluding Questions/Actions:
    a. What ideas do you have about the science conference?
    b. What investigation would you like to conduct?
    c. What else would you like to find out?

20. Ask students to date and write a new entry in their investigation lab books:
    a. When it comes to conducting scientific investigations, the most difficult thing is . . .
    b. The next investigation I would like conduct on matter is . . .

Extending the Lesson

What to Do at Home
  • Using your Wheel of Scientific Investigation and Reasoning, and with an adult's help, conduct an experiment of your own to answer one of two questions: Do ice cubes melt faster in the kitchen or in the bathroom? Does water boil faster in one pan than in another pan? Remember to write down the steps to the experiment.

Name:_____ Date:_____

Scientific Investigation Sheet

Solid or Liquid: _____

Question: Do the properties of a _____ stay the same when the size is changed?

My Hypothesis:_____

_____

_____

_____

Materials Needed: (List the materials you are using.)

- _____
- _____
- _____
- _____
- _____
- _____
- _____
- _____
- _____
- _____
- _____
- _____

Name:_____ Date:_____

Experiment Process

Steps I will take to conduct the experiment:

- Make observations about my solid or liquid and record the observations on my data chart.

- Observations include using my senses and testing whether or not the objects take the shape of a new container or remain intact.

- I will reduce the objects in size by either dumping some out, if a liquid, or cutting or breaking the solids.

- I will record my observations of the smaller parts on my data table.

- I will compare my results of the smaller parts with the results of the larger parts.

- I will write my conclusion and determine if my hypothesis was true.

My conclusion:

The properties of a

solid   **liquid**   **do**   **do not**

remain the same when reduced in size. (Circle answers above.)

My hypothesis was   **correct**   **incorrect.**   (Circle answer.)

Name:_____ Date:_____

Data Table: Part 1

	Observations *Before* Being Reduced in Size	Properties *Before* Being Reduced in Size (Did it take the shape of its container?)	
		Yes	No
Object 1:			
Object 2:			
Object 3:			
Object 4:			

Name:_____ Date:_____

Data Table: Part 2

	Observations *After* Being Reduced in Size	Properties *After* Being Reduced in Size (Did it take the shape of its container?)	
		Yes	No
Object 1:			
Object 2:			
Object 3:			
Object 4:			

Superintendent's Letter

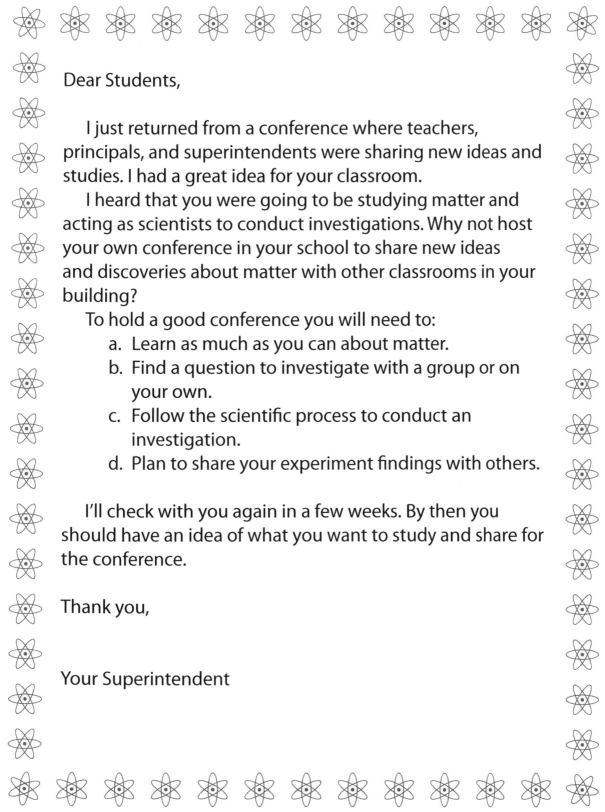

Dear Students,

    I just returned from a conference where teachers, principals, and superintendents were sharing new ideas and studies. I had a great idea for your classroom.

    I heard that you were going to be studying matter and acting as scientists to conduct investigations. Why not host your own conference in your school to share new ideas and discoveries about matter with other classrooms in your building?

    To hold a good conference you will need to:

    a. Learn as much as you can about matter.

    b. Find a question to investigate with a group or on your own.

    c. Follow the scientific process to conduct an investigation.

    d. Plan to share your experiment findings with others.

    I'll check with you again in a few weeks. By then you should have an idea of what you want to study and share for the conference.

Thank you,

Your Superintendent

Scientific Investigation Badges

I Conducted
a Scientific
Investigation—
Ask Me About It!

I Conducted
a Scientific
Investigation—
Ask Me About It!

I Conducted
a Scientific
Investigation—
Ask Me About It!

I Conducted
a Scientific
Investigation—
Ask Me About It!

I Conducted
a Scientific
Investigation—
Ask Me About It!

I Conducted
a Scientific
Investigation—
Ask Me About It!

Lesson 6:
The Case of the Mystery Goop

Planning the Lesson

Instructional Purposes: To understand the concept of molecules and how they act in solids, liquids, and gases; to investigate whether a mystery substance is a solid or a liquid based on the properties of matter and how molecules in matter are combined.

Instructional Time: 45 minutes

Essential Science Understandings:
- Matter is anything that has mass and takes up space.
- There are three states of matter: solids, liquids, and gases.
- Materials are composed of parts that are too small to see without magnification.

Scientific Investigation Skills and Processes:
- Make observations.
- Ask questions.
- Learn more.
- Tell others what was found.
- Make predictions.

Change Concept Generalizations:
- Change may be random or predictable.
- Change is everywhere.
- Change may be natural or manmade.

What to Look for in Assessment:
- Can students generate questions and select science concepts from the scenario provided?
- Can students articulate the properties of solids and liquids to solve a problem?
- Can students discuss that matter is made up of smaller parts that react differently, depending on the state of matter?

Materials/Resources/Equipment:
- Large area for students to move around (move the desks or go outside)
- One eyedropper with water for the class to share
- Word wall card: molecules
- Envelope with the Mystery Goop Letter (p. 73) inside
- Chart or transparency of the Properties of Matter Concept Map (p. 74) and the Wheel of Scientific Investigation and Reasoning (p. 55)
- For each student you will need:
    o 6 tsp cornstarch
    o 1 Tbsp water
    o Bowl
    o Zipper bag

o   Copies of Particles of Solids, Liquids, and Gases handout (p. 75)
o   Student lab books

Implementing the Lesson

Part I:
1. Open an envelope containing the Mystery Goop Letter (p. 73) Read the letter to the students yourself or ask the cafeteria manager from the school to read the letter to your class.
2. Show students the Wheel of Scientific Investigation and Reasoning (p. 55). Ask students to determine what questions they may have about the mystery substance. Write them on their paper or the back of the handout. Brainstorm a list of questions as a group based on what the students wrote.
3. Ask the students what the cafeteria manager needs to find out. (Is the substance a liquid or solid?)
4. Ask students to complete their hypothesis about the two questions at hand.
5. Ask students how they might test their hypothesis. After several ideas, help lead students toward recreating the substance to observe with their senses (except taste) how the substance acts.
6. Ask students to consider what ingredients were included in the manager's discovery (cornstarch and water that looked like mayonnaise). Give each student a bowl and some cornstarch and water. Ask them to add just a little bit of water to the cornstarch until it begins to look like mayonnaise. Once they have a good consistency, tell the students to observe the cornstarch and water by picking it up, squeezing it, scooping it, setting it back in the bowl, and so forth. (Usually 6 tsp. of cornstarch and 1 Tbsp. of water will be sufficient to create a good consistency. If the mixture gets too stiff, add a few drops of water with an eyedropper.)
7. After students have found the right consistency, the cornstarch mixture should liquefy and ooze through the student's fingers but solidify when squeezed. Once students have had time to discover how the mixture reacts ask the following questions:
   a.   What is the mixture?
   b.   What properties does the mixture have?
   c.   Does it act more like a solid, liquid, or gas?
   d.   How might we classify this mixture? Allow time for students to defend whether or not they believe the mixture is a solid or liquid.
   e.   What is happening to the mixture when we squeeze it?
   f.   What are we going to tell the cook?

8. Tell students to put their mixture in a baggie and clean up their area. Tell them you will help them figure out what is happening to the mixture. You might have some ideas that will help the cook out that have to do with things we cannot see.

Part II:
1. To review the three main states of matter with the students, complete the Properties of Matter Concept Map (p. 74); see Figure 4 below for examples. Use the following questions as a guide:
   a.   What does all matter have?
   b.   What does matter take up?
   c.   What are the properties you observed about solids? Liquids? Gases?

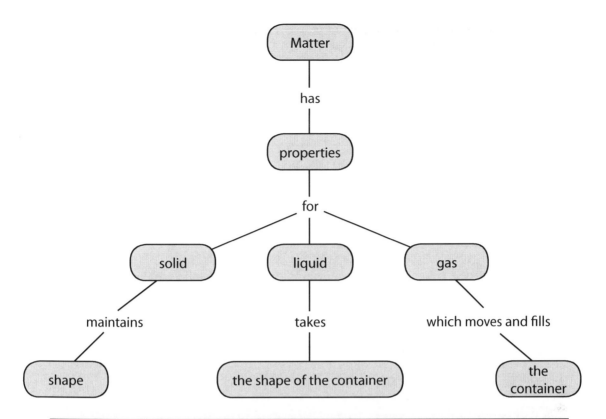

2. Remind students about the experiment with the paper towel and the glass. Even though we can't see air, we know it is there. Explain to students that while solid and liquid matter has many properties that we can observe with our five senses, there are also properties of matter that we cannot see. Write the word *molecules* and the following definition on the board: "a small particle, a tiny bit; the smallest particle of a substance that retains the chemical and physical properties of the substance."

3. Explain to students that molecules behave differently depending on whether they are part of a solid, a liquid, or a gas. Because we cannot see molecules, except with the use of a very strong microscope, we are going to use our bodies to demonstrate how molecules move within each state of matter.

   a. *Solid:* The particles that make up a solid are packed closely together and attracted to each other very strongly; they do not move around much. Choose 12 students to be the "molecules." Have three students stand side-by-side. Line up the remaining students in columns behind these students. The group of students should form a square. Have each student rest his or her left arm on the shoulder of the person in front of him or her and rest his or her right arm on the shoulder of the person to his or her right. In this formation, students represent the molecules of a solid, with their arms signifying the strong attractive forces that hold the molecules of a solid together. Solids are solid because their molecules are compact.

   b. *Liquid:* The particles that make up a liquid are attracted to each other a little bit less and move around more. Have a different group of students (about 10–12) stand together in a group. Tell them they can move around, pass each other, and changes places as long as they are always within touching distance of another student. This formation is like a liquid. Molecules are attracted to each other and remain fairly close, but they can slide past each other. Liquids take the shape of their containers because their molecules are loosely aligned.

    c. *Gas:* The particles that make up gas have the least attraction to each other and move around the most. Have another group of students (10–12) begin by standing in a group. Tell them they can go wherever they like and do not have to be within touching distance of another student. This is like the behavior of gas molecules.

4. Distribute Particles of Solids, Liquids, and Gases handout (p. 75). Have students complete the handout independently. Discuss individual answers with the whole class.

5. Once students have successfully completed the activity, ask them if anyone has ideas about what the cook's substance is and why it acts the way it does. Students should be able to explain that the new substance acted like both a liquid and a solid. When the substance was squeezed together quickly, the molecules in the goop were compacted and made it appear to be solid. Because cornstarch and water do not mix well, when you let go of the mixture it acts more like a thick liquid, meaning that the molecules relax and are not as compact as a solid. This is called a *suspension.* This means that the cornstarch and water do not really mix completely. Instead the cornstarch molecules glob together and are suspended in the water. Milk is another example of a suspension. Tell students to go home and add a few drops of milk to water and observe what happens.

6. Engage students in a discussion using the following questions as a guide.
    a. How did you use the Wheel of Scientific Investigation and Reasoning to figure out what the new substance was? Review the wheel components if necessary.
    b. How do you think the cook should dispose of the goop?
    c. How does the goop change if a lot of water is added?
    d. How does the goop change if more cornstarch is added?

7. Ask students if they can think of additional questions they might want to investigate for the Matter Conference. They should write their ideas in the marked section of the lab book. *Note:* Emphasize to students that even though the goop may act more like a liquid because it takes the shape of its container, they should never put anything down the sink except water unless they have permission. Dispose of the goop in the trashcan.

8. Concluding Questions/Actions:
    a. Ask students to help you make a list of science words (concepts) that were used in this lesson. Tell students to talk with a partner about these words and what each of the words means. Then ask for volunteers to use one of the words in a sentence that talks about something they learned in the lesson. Create a chart of sentences.
    b. Ask students to date and write a new entry in their student lab books: Write a letter or draw a diagram to show the cafeteria manager about molecules and the properties of solids, liquids, and gases. Share with a partner and compare your answers.

Extending the Lesson

What to Do at Home

- Show your mystery goop to your family. Explain about molecules of solids, liquids, gases, and suspensions. Lead your family through the activity we did in class to show them about solid, liquid, and gas molecules.
- Add a few drops of milk to a cup of water and watch what happens. Milk and water do not mix. The milk will suspend in the water. Explain why that happens. Ask your family if you can test other liquids to see if they suspend or mix. Make a table to record your results. Share them with the class.

Mystery Goop Letter

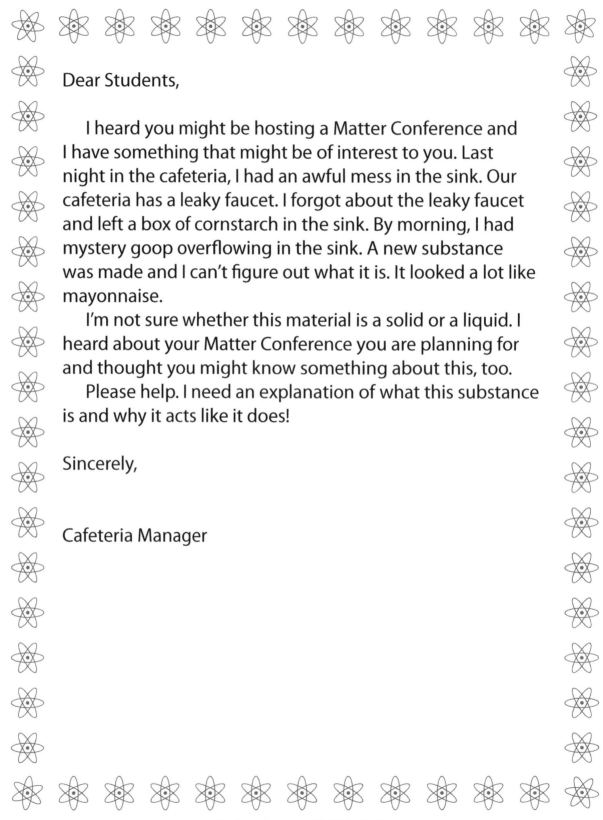

Dear Students,

    I heard you might be hosting a Matter Conference and I have something that might be of interest to you. Last night in the cafeteria, I had an awful mess in the sink. Our cafeteria has a leaky faucet. I forgot about the leaky faucet and left a box of cornstarch in the sink. By morning, I had mystery goop overflowing in the sink. A new substance was made and I can't figure out what it is. It looked a lot like mayonnaise.

    I'm not sure whether this material is a solid or a liquid. I heard about your Matter Conference you are planning for and thought you might know something about this, too.

    Please help. I need an explanation of what this substance is and why it acts like it does!

Sincerely,

Cafeteria Manager

Name:_____ Date:_____

Properties of Matter Concept Map

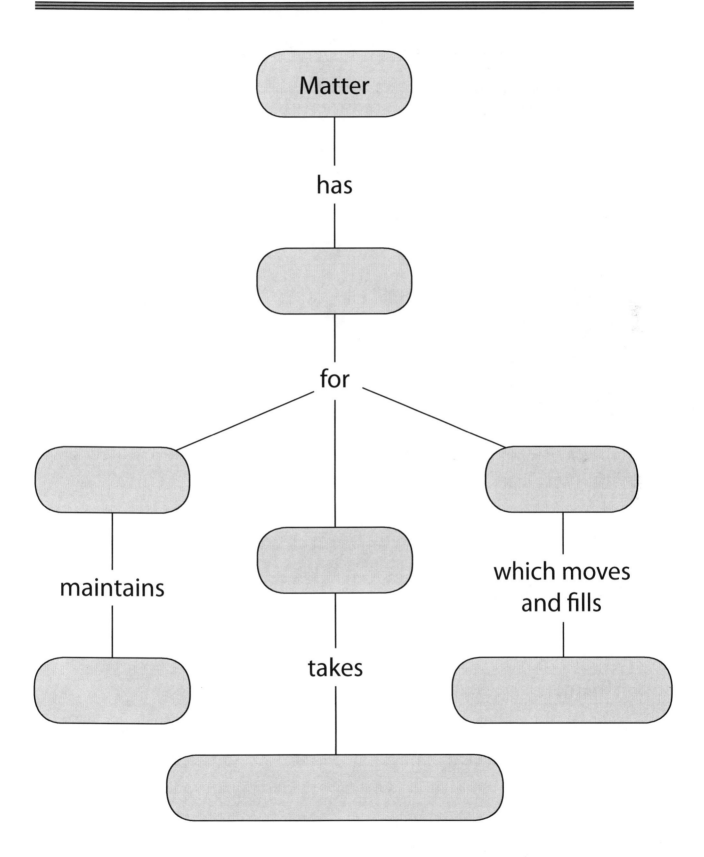

Matter

has

for

maintains   which moves
                                               and fills

takes

Name:_____ Date:_____

Particles of a Solids, Liquids, and Gases

Directions: Label each diagram as solid, liquid, or gas. Then answer the two questions below.

Particles in a	Particles in a	Particles in a
_____	_____	_____

Compare the particles in a solid to the particles in a liquid. How are they different?

_____

_____

_____

Compare the particles in a liquid to the particles in a gas. How are they different?

_____

_____

_____

Lesson 7:
Physical Changes by Changing Temperatures

Planning the Lesson

Instructional Purposes: To analyze the physical states of matter and the importance of removing or adding heat as part of the physical change; to make ice cream to demonstrate removal of heat in a change of matter.

Instructional Time: 45 minutes

Essential Science Understandings:
- Matter is anything that has mass and takes up space.
- Matter can change from one state to another; these changes are referred to as physical changes.
- Temperature and energy can create physical changes in matter.
- Materials are composed of parts that are too small to see without magnification.

Scientific Investigation Skills and Processes:
- Learn more.
- Tell others what was found.

Change Concept Generalizations:
- Change is related to time.
- Change can be natural or manmade.

What to Look for in Assessment:
- Can students explain how temperature affects matter?
- Can students explain a physical change?
- Can students articulate how change is related to the investigation?
- Can students articulate how molecules react during temperature changes in the varied states of matter?

Materials/Resources/Equipment:
- Zipper bag with 3–4 chocolate chips or small chocolate bar for each student or small group
- One large coffee can or plastic jar per group of 3–4 students
- Quart-size zipper bag (One per group)
- Half-and-half cream, enough for ½ cup per group
- Crushed ice, enough to fill each coffee can half full
- Transparency of Directions for Making Ice Cream (p. 80)

> **Teacher's Note:** Students make ice cream in this activity by combining ingredients and rolling the coffee can to freeze the cream. You may want to enlist volunteer help to prepare for and supervise this activity.

- Salt, preferably rock salt, at least 6 Tbsp per can
- Vanilla extract (artificial is fine), ½ tsp per group
- Sugar, 1 Tbsp per group
- Towel (or winter gloves) for each group
- Student lab book
- Word wall cards: freezing point, melting point, heat, energy, physical change, and chemical change

Implementing the Lesson

1. Remind students of the investigation they conducted to learn that the properties of matter stay the same, even if the size changes. Ask students to predict whether or not matter stays the same when the temperature changes. Allow time for students to discuss their predictions.
2. Explain to students that matter can go through *physical and chemical* changes. Explain that a physical change occurs when matter changes from one state to another but remains the same matter. A chemical change occurs when matter changes to create something new (e.g., mixing ingredients to bake a cake—you can't get the mixed ingredients back).
3. Tell students that water is the most commonly used example to demonstrate physical changes in matter.
   a. What do you predict will happen to ice that is left out in the room? (It will melt.)
   b. What about water that is put in the freezer? (It will become ice.)
   c. What causes water to change from solid to liquid? (Heat.)
   d. Where does the heat come from to melt the ice? (The air in the room.)
   e. How does water change from a liquid to a gas? What's an example they might think of? (Boiling water at home.)
   f. When ice turns to water vapor, is it still water? (Yes, just in a different state of matter.)

4. Give students a baggie of chocolate chips or a small chocolate bar. Ask students to determine the state of matter. Next, ask students to hold the baggie with chocolate in their palms for about a minute. Ask students to set the chocolate baggie on their desk and observe what is happening to the chocolate. They should notice that the chocolate is beginning to melt. Ask students the following questions:
   a. What difference did holding the chocolate in your hand make?
   b. What might have happened if you just left the chocolate on your desk? What if you put it under a heat lamp? What if you placed in the freezer?
   c. When the chocolate melted, did it change in to something else or is it still chocolate?
   d. What can you infer about change in states of matter?
   e. Is the chocolate still chocolate even if it is melted or frozen? Is the melting chocolate a physical or chemical change? Why?

5. Students should begin to infer that changes in matter occur based on temperature or heat and energy changes. Ask students if they've ever left crayons in their car on a hot summer day. What happened? Was that a physical or chemical change? (*Note*: After this discussion is complete, make certain that the students understand that this is not something that they should intentionally do. Melted crayons can be difficult if not impossible to remove from carpet/upholstery.)

6. Assign students to small groups and tell them that they will now conduct another investigation to find out what happens to matter when the temperature changes.
7. Show students the ice, salt, cream, sugar, and vanilla. Ask them to identify the state of matter of each. Explain that they are going to change the temperature of liquids by adding ice.
8. Guide student groups (3–4 students per group) through the process of making ice cream using the Directions for Making Ice Cream (p. 80). The zipper bags can be prepared ahead of time.
9. Tell students to return to their group seats and carefully open their can or jar. Then, tell them to remove the zipper bag. Ask students the following questions:
    a. What happened to the cream mixture?
    b. What happened to the ice and salt mixture?
    c. Was your hypothesis correct?

10. Rinse off the bags with water to get rid of the salt. Give each student a spoon and a small plastic cup in which to scoop and enjoy their homemade ice cream. You or adult volunteers should rinse the bags and discard of the contents of the coffee cans.
11. While students are eating their ice cream, ask students what the effect was of lowering the temperature of a liquid. Explain that temperature is very important when changing the physical state of matter.
12. Ask students why they think salt needed to be added to the ice. Tell them to think about what happens in colder places in the wintertime when salt is added to a road before or after it snows. Explain that adding the salt causes some of the ice to melt because salt lowers the *freezing point* of ice. In order for the ice to melt, it must absorb heat. Heat is absorbed from the cream mixture. Explain that heat is a form of *energy*.
13. Ask students to recall what they remember about the molecules of solids, liquids, and gases. In what state of matter are the molecules close together? Far apart? In-between? Draw these examples on the board.
14. Explain that adding heat to a solid adds energy to the molecules, which causes them to speed up and move farther apart, turning the matter into a liquid. Ask students where the heat from the experiment came from to melt the ice. (The air is warmer than the ice and it started to melt with the help of the salt). Explain that melting happens when the particles of the solid reach a certain temperature, called the *melting point*. Conversely, removing heat from a liquid removes energy from the molecules, which causes them to slow down and move closer together, turning the liquid to a solid. Freezing happens when the particles of the liquid reach a certain temperature, called the *freezing point*. Ask students to explain which part of the experiment included a freezing. (The cream mixture.)
15. Finally, tell students they have witnessed both a physical change and a chemical change. A physical change happened when the ice melted. A physical change is when the matter changes states but remains the same type of matter; in other words nothing new is formed. A chemical change is a change that happens when different matter is combined to create something new. Ask students to identify the example of the chemical change in the experiment. (Cream mixture turning into ice cream. The cream mixture cannot return to its individual parts.)
16. Read aloud these questions concerning change generalizations:
    a. Is this change in the liquid natural or caused by people?
    b. When and how could it be both?
    c. How does this change fit with the generalization "Change relates to time?"

17. Concluding Questions/Actions:

a. How does heat affect the particles of a solid?
b. How does cold affect the particles of a liquid?
c. What do you think happens to a liquid when heat is added? Give an example.
d. What is the difference between a physical and chemical change?
e. What was the purpose of today's experiment?
f. In today's experiment, we observed a change in matter from one state to another. Explain this change. How did it happen?
g. Which generalization of change applies to our findings?
h. Do you have additional ideas for the Matter Conference? Write your ideas in your lab book.

18. Ask students to date and write a new entry in their investigation lab books:
a. Explain the importance of temperature and the physical properties of matter.

Directions for Making Ice Cream

Materials:
- Metal coffee can or large plastic jar
- Quart-size zipper bags
- Crushed ice
- Rock salt
- Half-and-half or milk
- Sugar
- Vanilla
- Teaspoons
- Tablespoons
- Measuring cups
- Towels or gloves to protect student hands

Instructions:
1. Fill the coffee can or plastic jar half full with crushed ice.
2. Add 4–6 Tbsp of rock salt to the ice. Seal the can or jar and roll around for 1–3 minutes.
3. Make an observation of what you see happening to the can or jar. Record your observations in your science log.
4. As the cans or jars get really cold to the touch, you may need to wrap a towel around it to protect your hands.
5. Add the following ingredients to the zipper bag: ½ cup of half-and-half or milk, 1 Tbsp of sugar, and ½ tsp of vanilla.
6. Squeeze as much air as possible out of the bag and seal it tightly.
7. Place the bag inside the can or jar and seal it tightly.
8. Make a hypothesis about what you think will happen to the ice and to the liquid mixture. Hypotheses should be noted on the board.
9. The jars or cans should be rolled for 6–9 minutes. The mixture should be checked every 3–4 minutes. Spare towels also can be used to catch and clean up minor leaks from the cans.

Lesson 8:
Who Stole the Principal's Water?

Planning the Lesson

Instructional Purposes: To examine and investigate the importance of temperature on the molecules of solids, liquids, and gases; to understand evaporation by trying to figure out what happened to salt water in the principal's office.

Instructional Time: 45 minutes

Essential Science Understandings:
- Matter is anything that has mass and takes up space.
- Matter can change from one state to another; these changes are referred to as physical changes.
- Temperature and energy can create physical changes in matter.
- Materials are composed of parts that are too small to see without magnification.

Scientific Investigation Skills and Processes:
- Make observations.
- Ask questions.
- Learn more.

What to Look for in Assessment:
- Can students accurately demonstrate how molecules react when heat is added or taken away?
- Can students explain what happens to a gas when heat is removed?

Materials/Resources/Equipment:
- 4–6 gram cubes for each student
- Empty water bottle with a cap and access to the school cafeteria freezer
- Transparency or copies of Changes in Matter Concept Map, Changes in the States of Matter, and Need-to-Know Chart (pp. 84–86) for each student
- Transparency of Principal's Letter (p. 87)
- Student lab book

Implementing the Lesson

1. Tell students: "We are going to create a new concept map about matter." Show students a transparency of the Changes in Matter Concept Map (p. 84) and make copies for student use. Use the concept map below (see Figure 5), as well as the following questions to guide students in completing the concept map.
    a. What did we learn about matter yesterday?
    b. What are some of the types of change that matter goes through?
    c. How is matter changed?
    d. What happens to the molecules of the matter when it melts? When it freezes?

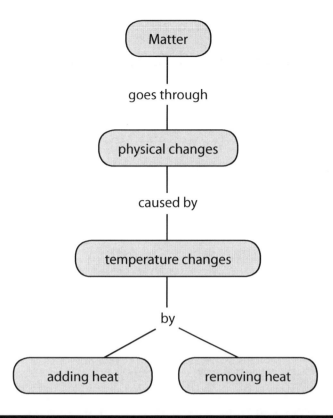

Figure 5. Example of concept map on matter.

   e. What about the temperature? (Students should explain the importance of temperature and that heat must be added or removed.)
   f. What is a physical change is and how it is created?

2. Ask students if all types of matter go through physical changes when heat is added or removed. Explain that each object has a different melting point and boiling point, but eventually when enough heat is added or removed the matter will change states.
3. Ask students what they know about temperature changes in a gas. Ask students to brainstorm with a partner at least 10 ways they might figure out what happens when a gas changes temperature.
4. Collect an empty water or soda bottle with a lid. Take your students on a walk to the cafeteria freezer. As you are walking to the cafeteria, make sure your students understand that there is gas in the empty bottle. Remind them about the paper towel and balloon in the bottle demonstrations and how gas takes up space.
5. Place the bottle in the freezer for approximately 2 minutes. While you wait, ask students to predict what will happen to the gas in the bottle when it is frozen. How do they know? (Help students consider what molecules of matter do when they get cold or hot.)
6. Take the bottle out of the freezer. The bottle should be partially collapsed. Ask students to think about why this would happen while you walk back to your classroom.
7. Discuss student explanations.
8. Divide students into groups of 2–3 and give each a stack of gram cubes. Review the behavior of particles of a solid and a liquid with gram cubes, asking the following questions:

a. How could you represent a solid? Have students create a solid cube of blocks. What is the volume of your solid?

b. Now pretend we are going to add heat to your solid. What happens? How could you represent a liquid using the cubes? Make sure that their cubes are not stacked on top of each other, are disconnected, and are a little distance apart.

c. Finally, pretend more heat is added. What state is your matter in now? Represent a gas with the gram cubes. Make sure that the cubes are further apart than in the liquid.

9. Distribute Changes in the States of Matter handout (p. 85). Instruct students to complete it based on what they know about matter when heat is added or removed. Students should place dots as molecules either far apart or close together. Above the arrow line they should write whether heat is added or removed.

10. As students complete this handout, ask the principal to meet you in the classroom to read the Principal's Letter (p. 87). Have the principal read or explain it in his or her own words.

11. After the principal leaves, explain that you have something that may help the students organize their thoughts. Display an overhead and distribute a copy of the Need-to-Know Chart (p. 86).

12. Tell students to talk with a partner about what they know so far about the mystery. They may discuss or write their ideas under the "What Do We Know?" column of the handout. Discuss what you know as a whole group. As students share ideas, make sure their ideas are written in the first column. Sometimes students make inferences about what they think they know, even though it wasn't explicit. (Students should be able to determine that the water was shallow, there was something in the bottom, and that the ocean water is salty. They also may note that the principal's office is rather warm and that the water was in the windowsill and therefore exposed to sun.)

13. Follow the same procedure for the second and third columns: What Do We Need to Know? How Can We Find Out?

14. Tell the students you will finish discussing their ideas the following day. Encourage them to talk to their parents about how they might conduct an investigation to find out what happened to the water.

15. To conclude the lesson, ask students to date and write a new entry in their investigation lab books:

a. Do you think someone really stole the principal's water or do you think there is another explanation? Explain your answer.

Extending the Lesson

What to Do at Home

- Demonstrate the collapsing bottle trick at home. Explain what happens to molecules when gases get cold. What happens if you rinse the bottle with hot water and then put it in the freezer? What happens if you do not put the lid on the bottle and then put it in the freezer?

Changes in Matter Concept Map

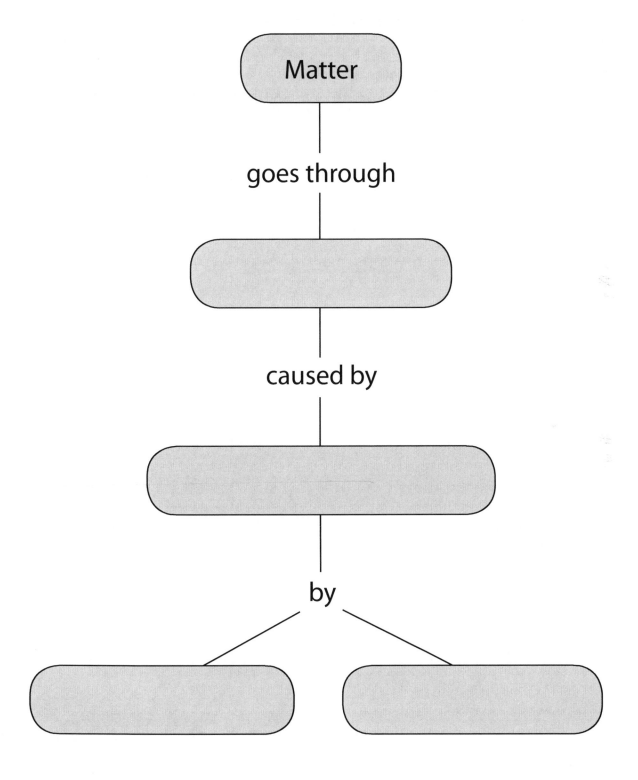

Matter

goes through

caused by

by

Name:_____ Date:_____

Changes in the States of Matter

What happens to molecules of matter when there is a change in temperature? Draw the molecules for liquids, solids, or gases in each box below, as listed by the label. Above each arrow, write whether heat must be added or removed to change the state from the property in the left box to that in the right box.

Liquid   **Solid**

Liquid   **Gas**

Solid   **Liquid**

Name: _____   Date: _____

Need-to-Know Chart

What Do We Know?	What Do We Need to Know?	How Can We Find Out?

Principal's Letter

Dear Students,

I went on a trip to the ocean this summer. I wanted a souvenir, so I gathered a cup full of ocean water. I took the ocean water back to my office and poured it into a shallow container to leave on my window as a decoration and memory of my trip. I think someone stole my water. It was there all week, but when I returned after the weekend the water was gone! The container was still there but no water was in the container. There was a little bit of dust in the bottom. It might be a clue.

I know you've been doing some investigating recently and you're planning a Matter Conference. Could you help me investigate this problem? I need to know if someone stole my salt water or if there is a more scientific explanation.

Sincerely,

Your Principal

P.S. Enjoy your room being so cool. My office is quite warm.

Lesson 9:
Who Stole the Principal's Water?
Part II

Planning the Lesson

Instructional Purposes: To investigate who stole the principal's ocean water based on what was learned from the previous lesson; to begin planning an independent investigation on matter for the Matter Conference.

Instructional Time: 45 minutes

Essential Science Understandings:
- Matter is anything that has mass and takes up space.
- Matter can change from one state to another; these changes are referred to as physical changes.
- Temperature and energy can create physical changes in matter.
- Materials are composed of parts that are too small to see without magnification.
- Some solids will dissolve in water, and more quickly in hot than cold water.

Scientific Investigation Skills and Processes:
- Make observations.
- Ask questions.
- Learn more.
- Design and conduct experiments.
- Create meaning.
- Tell others what was found.

Change Concept Generalization:
- Change is everywhere.

What to Look for in Assessment:
- Can students follow directions to complete the experimental steps?
- Can students understand how to record data using a data table?
- Can students use scientific words from the word wall in conversation?

Materials/Resources/Equipment:
- Need-to-Know Charts from the previous lesson (p. 86)
- Metal pie pan, ⅓ cup of very warm water, spoon, and heaping teaspoon of salt for each group of students
- Cup of cold water in a clear glass and a heaping teaspoon of salt
- Permanent marker
- Thermometer for each group
- Copies of Experimental Design, Ocean Water Data Log, and Matter Conference Experiment handouts (pp. 91–94) for each student
- Transparency of Superintendent's Letter and Questions for the Matter Conference (pp. 97–98)

- Student lab books
- Word wall card: dissolve

Teacher's Note: Read students' lab book entries about their ideas for the Matter Conference and provide feedback for student experiments. Place students with similar ideas together in a group as appropriate. Begin helping students plan their experiments.

Implementing the Lesson

1. Briefly review the previous lesson with students.
2. Ask them if they have any other ideas for the principal. Provide or allow time for students to investigate some of the topical questions from the "What Do I Need to Know?" column.
3. Help students understand that they need to re-create the scene as closely as possible.
4. Review what you know: shallow pan, saltwater, near window, warm, water was there on Monday but gone the following Monday.
5. Divide students into groups. Give each group of students a shallow metal pie pan, a heaping teaspoon of salt, ⅓ cup of very warm water, and a spoon. Tell students to write their group name on the outside of the pie pan. Mix the salt and the water together, stirring the water until the salt disappears. Ask the students what happened to the salt. Explain that they just created a *solution* of a solid and liquid: two different states of matter. After students have stirred the salt into the water, dump it into the pie pan so that the mixture is rather shallow but covers the bottom of the pan. Salt should be completely mixed. Explain to students that even though they can't see the salt, it is still there. They may want to place their finger in the water to taste the salt.
6. Ask the students why the water you gave them was warm. What would happen if you used cold water to dissolve the salt? In a clear glass or cup, pour some cold water and add salt. Allow students to observe the difference between how their salt dissolved and how salt in cold water dissolves. Students should conclude that the warmer the water, the more quickly solids will dissolve.
7. If available, ask the principal to come to the room and examine the pie pans and mixture. Allow the students to explain that they are re-creating the scene to see what happened. The principal may be able to answer other questions the students might have and examine their mixtures to ensure that they are similar to what he or she had.
8. Allow students to place their mixture in the window. (If it is cold out, remind the students that they need heat. (You may need to place a lamp over the mixture to add heat, if necessary.)
9. Tell students they need to observe the mixture every day for the next week and record their observations in a data table or log. Brainstorm with students what might be important to observe.
10. Students may create their own tables and logs in their lab book or use the Experimental Design (pp. 91–92) or Ocean Water Data Log (p. 93) handouts.
11. Throughout the next week, allow students a couple of minutes each day to record their observations.
12. By the third or fourth day, students may notice that the water level is slowly going down and there is a white coating on the bottom of the pan. If not, apply more heat.
13. Continue to the next two lessons while students record data. Go to Lesson 12 once the experiment is concluded and the water has evaporated. Depending on the temperature, this could take less than 7 days.
14. In the meantime, ask students if they have been thinking about what they might want to investigate for the Matter Conference. Ask them to look through their lab

book. With the class, brainstorm a list of questions students still have about matter. Ask them which of the questions are testable. How?

15. Show or read the Superintendent's Letter (p. 97). Explain that you received another letter from the superintendent.

16. Look at the questions listed on the board. Show Questions for Matter Conference (p. 98) and ask students how their questions align with the questions on the overhead. Explain that some of the questions haven't been discussed yet in this unit. Tell students they should select a question and experiment steps for their conference presentation by the end of the week. They also may work with a partner or in groups if they choose.

17. Distribute the Matter Conference Experiment handout (p. 94–96) to the class. Explain that as the students are considering what they will do for the Matter Conference they should be following the template provided. After they write their conclusion, students should be able to explain in scientific terms what happened. They may use the words on the word wall as a guide. Tell students they also must think about how they will best demonstrate their experiment's findings to the audience. For example, they could do a poster of their findings, a PowerPoint presentation, or a demonstration.

18. To conclude the lesson, ask students to date and write a new entry in their investigation lab books:

    a. Explain what you are considering for the Matter Conference. What is your question? How will you find out the answer? Do you want to work by yourself or with another person?

Extending the Lesson

What to Do at Home

- Tell your parents about the Matter Conference. Tell them your ideas for an investigation. Ask them if they have other ideas or suggestions. Be prepared to share in class.

Name:_____ Date:_____

Experimental Design

Experiment name: Case of the Missing Ocean Water

My question: _____

_____

_____

_____

_____

_____

My hypothesis: _____

_____

_____

_____

_____

_____

Materials needed:

- _____
- _____
- _____
- _____
- _____
- _____
- _____

Steps needed for the experiment:

1. _____

2. _____

3. _____

4. _____

5. _____

6. _____

7. _____

8. _____

Conclusion based on hypothesis: _____

_____

_____

_____

_____

_____

_____

Name:_____ Date:_____

Ocean Water Data Log

Day	Temperature	Observations of Salt Water
Day 1		
Day 2		
Day 3		
Day 4		
Day 5		
Day 6		
Day 7		

Name:_____ Date:_____

Matter Conference Experiment

My question: _____

_____

_____

_____

_____

My hypothesis: _____

_____

_____

_____

_____

Materials needed:

- _____
- _____
- _____
- _____
- _____
- _____
- _____
- _____

Steps for the experiment:

1. _____

2. _____

3. _____

4. _____

5. _____

6. _____

7. _____

8. _____

My data:

- _____

- _____

- _____

- _____

- _____

- _____

- _____

- _____

Conclusion based on hypothesis: _____

_____

_____

_____

_____

_____

What I learned: _____

_____

_____

_____

_____

_____

_____

_____

_____

_____

_____

_____

_____

Superintendent's Letter

Dear Students,

By now you should know more about matter and have a better idea of some investigations you can conduct on your own or with a group. I look forward to seeing your investigations and findings at the Matter Conference.

I have talked with your teacher and we came up with a list of questions to help you with an investigation. You also may use a question of your own. Just be sure to get it approved by your teacher.

Keep up the great work.

Signed,

Your Superintendent

Questions for the Matter Conference

- Do properties of a solid remain the same when the size is increased?

- Does the mass of a liquid change when it undergoes a physical change?

- Do all liquids have the same freezing point?

- Do all liquids evaporate at the same rate?

- Which type of soda has the most gas?

- Are mass and size related?

- Does the volume of a liquid change if it is placed in a different container?

- Does the starting amount of water in a container make a difference when measuring the volume of a solid by water displacement?

- Does the temperature make a difference in the rate of evaporation of water?

- Do solids dissolve better in cold water or hot water?

Lesson 10:
Measuring Mass

Planning the Lesson

Instructional Purposes: To measure the mass of matter in solids and liquids by using a balance; to conduct a simple investigation to determine if the mass of an ice cube stays the same when it melts.

Instructional Time: 45 minutes

Essential Science Understandings:
- Mass is a measure of the amount of matter.
- There are three states of matter: solids, liquids, and gases.
- All common substances are made of matter.
- Matter is anything that has mass and takes up space.
- Matter can change from one state to another; these changes are referred to as physical changes.

Scientific Investigation Skills and Processes:
- Make observations.
- Ask questions.
- Learn more.
- Design and conduct experiments.
- Create meaning.
- Tell others what was found.

Change Concept Generalizations:
- Change is linked to time.
- Change can be natural or manmade.
- Change can be random or predictable.
- Change is everywhere.

What to Look for in Assessment:
- Can students use the balance to determine which of two objects has a greater mass?
- Can students use the balance correctly to measure and graph the mass of solid and liquid objects?
- Can students determine that mass and weight are different?
- Can students determine that mass and size may not be the same?
- Can students articulate that the mass of an object remains the same when the physical state changes?

Materials/Resources/Equipment:
- Two glasses of the same size
- Water
- Ice cube

- Balance with plastic containers on each side that allows measurement of mass of liquids (one for every 4–6 students; groups can be made larger if there are not enough balances)
- Word wall card: mass
- Set of plastic mass cubes, weighing 1 gram each (unifix cubes also may work if you do not have mass cubes)
- A collection of small items such as a penny, a crayon, a pair of children's scissors, and a small paper cup with 20 milliliters of water (one set of these items for each group)
- Copies of Using a Balance, Comparing Mass, and Investigation Record Sheet handouts (pp. 103–106)
- Student lab books

Implementing the Lesson

1. Review with students the different properties of matter that they have discovered thus far during their scientific investigations. Explain to students that in addition to the properties they have already discovered, all matter has mass. On the board, write the following definition of mass: "a measure of how much matter there is in an object."

2. Mass is one of the physical properties of an object. Explain that mass is similar to weight, but they are not exactly the same. Weight is a combination of mass and gravity. Different places, such as the earth and the moon, have different strengths of gravity. On the moon, an apple will weigh less than it does on earth. However, its mass, or the amount of *matter* in the apple, will remain the same.

3. Explain to students that mass may not be related to size. Blow up a balloon as large as it can go without popping. Set the balloon beside a thick book. Ask students which object is bigger. Then ask students which object has the most mass. Students should realize that even though the balloon is bigger in size, the book has more mass or is made of more matter.

4. Mass is measured by using a balance, whereas weight is measured using a scale. A balance works a lot like a seesaw: when the mass of an object on one side of the balance is equal to the mass of an object on the other side of the balance, the balance will be level. Have each student refer to his or her copy of the Using a Balance handout (p. 103) as you demonstrate with a balance the class can see. The balances each hold two containers: A and B.

5. Put two objects of equal mass in each of the containers in your demonstration scale. It will be helpful to find things of different sizes that balance to illustrate the point that mass may be the same even though the size may be different. Ask students to look at your scale and identify which picture on their paper it is most like. Ask students:
   a. What inferences can you make about the mass of these two objects?

6. Guide students to the conclusion that the mass of the two objects is equal. Instruct students to draw an equal sign (=) between A and B in the middle picture on their handout. Then ask them to complete exercise 1 on their handout.

7. Ask students to make predictions about the changes in the scale when an object is removed.
   a. What do you predict will happen when I remove the object in container B? Draw your prediction in the box below Exercise 2.
   b. What do you predict will happen when I remove the object in container A? Draw your prediction in the box below Exercise 3.

8. Once students have made their predictions, remove the item from container B and allow students to check the accuracy of their predictions. Repeat the process by replacing the item in container B and removing the item in container A.

9. Ask students to pick two small objects in the room. Have them vote on which has more mass. Have one student come to the front of the room and use the teacher's balance to determine if the prediction is correct. Do this several times until students have a good grasp of the workings of the balance. Tell them that next they will use the balance to measure the mass of an object.

10. Students will use the balance to measure the mass of an object by using weights of standard mass. Explain that the object to be measured is placed on one side of the balance. Then, objects of known mass, such as the gram cubes, are placed on the other side until the balance is level.

11. Demonstrate this using first a solid object in the classroom and then a small cup of water. Tell each group they will be creating a data table to record the mass of the following objects: a penny, a crayon, children's scissors, and a small paper cup with an ice cube in it. Tell students to measure the ice cube first and then leave it in the cup on the table for a different investigation. Students should measure the mass of each object by adding gram cubes to the opposite side until the balance is level. The actual mass of each object should be recorded on the Comparing Mass handout (pp. 104–105) as a graph. Help students determine how to complete the graph by coloring in the appropriate number of boxes to indicate the weight for each object. Students will need to write the unit measure on the vertical portion of the graph before completing it. Ensure that students are coloring in the graph correctly. Discuss their responses as follows:
    a. What might you infer from your data?
    b. Which object has the most mass? Does this surprise you? Why or why not?

12. Give students a ball of play dough. Ask them to determine the mass. Then ask them to predict what would happen if they changed the shape of the play dough from a ball to an animal. Would the mass change? What is their hypothesis? How might they test their hypothesis? Allow time for students to make something different out of the play dough. Measure the mass. Discuss their findings.

13. Ask students if they think an ice cube will have the same mass when it melts. How might they find out? Solicit responses. Distribute the Investigation Record Sheet (pp. 106–107) and discuss ideas for an investigation. Tell them to look at the Comparing Mass handout and record the mass of the ice cube. Check the ice cube to make sure it melted. Instruct students to determine the mass of the water and record. Discuss as follows:
    a. Does the mass of an object change when it undergoes a physical change? How do you know?
    b. Usually scientists repeat experiments to make sure they are correct. Because we did not repeat our experiment, how might we know we are correct? (Students should compare their results with others in the class. Did everyone have similar findings? Explain any differences and similarities.)
    c. Do you think your findings are true for all types of matter? How could you find out?

14. Concluding Questions and/or Actions:
    a. What does mass measure? (How much matter an object has.)
    b. What change generalizations apply to today's lesson?

c. If you and a friend each sat on one side of a seesaw, and the seesaw was lower on your side, what conclusion could you make about who has more mass, you or your friend?

d. What is the relationship between mass and shape? How do you know? How could you test it?

e. Does today's lesson change your experiment ideas? What additional ideas do you have? Write them in your lab book idea section.

15. To conclude the lesson, ask students to date and write a new entry in their lab books, answering the following:

a. The words *massive* and *amass* are related to the word *mass*. Define these two words and tell how their meaning is related to the meaning of mass.

b. Are mass and size related? Explain your answer.

Extending the Lesson

What to Do at Home

- Do a scavenger hunt at home to determine the following:

  a. What is the largest object in your house with the least amount of mass?

  b. What is the smallest object in your house with the least amount of mass?

  c. What is the largest object in your house with the greatest amount of mass?

  d. What is the smallest object in your house with the greatest amount of mass?

- Explain to your parents how mass, size, and weight are different.

- In the United States, we use pounds to measure the weight of people and objects. In most other countries, however, weight is measured in kilograms (there are 1,000 grams in one kilogram. Imagine 1,000 cubes stacked up—that would be one kilogram!). Using a bathroom scale, find out how much you weigh. Visit the following Web site to convert your weight in pounds to your weight in kilograms.

  a. http://www.paulnoll.com/Oregon/Canning/number-weight.html

- For an extra challenge, figure out how many gram cubes you would need to equal your mass in kilograms. (Remember, one kilogram equals 1,000 grams.)

Name:_____ Date:_____

Using a Balance

Using these examples, draw your prediction of what the scale will do for each experiment in the boxes.

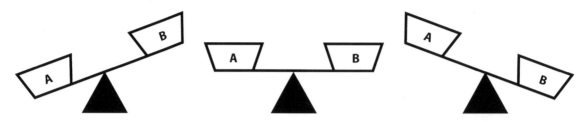

1. Show A and B having the same mass. Draw the balance.

2. The object in B is removed. Draw the balance.

3. The object in A is removed. Draw the balance.

Name:_____ Date:_____

Comparing Mass

In the box below, draw a graph that shows the mass of the following common items: a penny, a crayon, children's scissors, and an ice cube in a paper cup. Color in the boxes for each item to represent its mass in grams.

Graphing the Mass of Common Items

Grams	Penny	Crayon	Scissors	Ice Cube

My conclusion:

_____

_____

_____

_____

_____

_____

_____

_____

_____

_____

_____

_____

Investigation Record Sheet

My question: Does the mass of a solid change when it undergoes a physical change?

My hypothesis: _____

_____

_____

_____

_____

Materials:
- Ice cube
- Balance

Steps:
1. Measure the mass of the ice cube and record.
2. Allow time for the same ice cube to melt. Observe.
3. Measure the same melted ice cube.
4. Record the data on the table on the next page.
5. Write conclusions.

My Data:

Grams	**Ice Cube**	**Water**

My conclusion:

_____

_____

_____

_____

_____

_____

_____

_____

_____

_____

Lesson 11:
Measuring Volume

Planning the Lesson

Instructional Purpose: To measure the volume of two types of matter: solids and liquids.

Instructional Time: 45 minutes

Essential Science Understandings:
- Matter is anything that has mass and takes up space.
- Volume is the measure of the amount of space occupied by matter.

Scientific Investigation Skills and Processes:
- Make observations.
- Collect, classify, and analyze data.
- Create data tables.
- Draw inferences.
- Communicate findings.

Change Concept Generalizations:
- Change is everywhere.
- Change can be natural or manmade.

What to Look for in Assessment:
- Are students using the correct technique to measure a liquid?
- Are students arriving at accurate measurements of the water they are given to measure?
- Are students recording data promptly and accurately?
- Are students making correct inferences?

Materials/Resources/Equipment:
- Bottle (with label removed) of soda, juice, colored water, or other drink
- Plastic mass cubes (enough for each group to have about 30)
- Graduated plastic measuring cups in three sizes (1 cup, 2 cup, and 4 cup) with cup markings on one side and milliliter markings on the other side (enough for each group of 3–4 students to have one of each size)
- Metric rulers, 1 per student
- Bottles or pitchers of water, one per group
- A clear cup
- Four small stones or marbles per group
- Copies of Measuring Volume, Units of Volume, and Volume Investigation (pp. 113–115) for each student
- Student lab books

Implementing the Lesson

1. In this lesson students will be learning how to measure volume. The volume of matter is the amount of space that it takes up.

2. Give each student a mass cube. Have the students measure all sides of their cube. Each measures 1 centimeter. Tell students that the volume of the cube is 1 centimeter cubed or 1 cubic centimeter (which means 1 centimeter times 1 centimeter times 1 centimeter). Attach a second mass cube to the first. Ask the class what the volume of the structure just formed is. (2 cubic centimeters.) Attach two more mass cubes. What is the volume of the new structure? (4 cubic centimeters.) Review with students that because each mass cube has a volume of 1 cubic centimeter, they can determine the volume of any structure made of mass cubes by counting the number of mass cubes.

3. Have students break into groups of 3–4 for the following activity to reinforce this concept.

4. Give each group about 30 mass cubes and tell them to make a structure using as many cubes as they want and to put any unused cubes away. When they have finished making a structure, they should determine its volume by counting the number of cubes and record the volume on the Measuring Volume handout (p. 113) next to Structure 1. Then ask students to make a different structure using the same number of cubes and to determine and record the volume of the new structure on the handout next to Structure 2.

5. Convene students into a whole-class group for discussion. Use the following questions to stimulate a classroom discussion:
   a. What effect did changing the shape have? (Regardless of shape, they all have the same volume as long as they have the same number of cubes.)
   b. What does this finding tell you about volume? (Changing the shape of a solid does not change its volume.)
   c. If you were asked to make a structure using 50 mass cubes, what would its volume be? (50 centimeters cubed.) How did you find your answer?
   d. Is change in volume an example of a predictable or random change? Why?

6. Next, students will learn to measure the volume of a liquid. Tell students that they probably have a good idea how to measure the volume of a liquid already.

7. To precisely measure the volume of a liquid, we use a container that has measurement markings on the side. This is called a *graduated container*. Have students form their groups and give each group a plastic measuring cup. Have students look at the cup and at the markings on the side. Draw their attention to the line marked 1 cup. Review with them the other markings.

8. Pour some water into the cup (adding blue food coloring will make it easier for students to see in the graduated cylinder) and ask someone to demonstrate how to measure the volume of water in the cup. Elicit suggestions until it has been established that first you pour the liquid into the measuring cup. In order to measure accurately, students should also be told to:
   a. Place the measuring container on a flat surface.
   b. Place their eyes at the same level as the top of the water.

   Demonstrate this technique for students.

9. Leave students in groups, but address the whole class. Remind students that the United States uses different units of measurement than most other countries. U.S. customary units of volume are the cup, pint, quart, and gallon. Have students refer to the Units of Volume handout (p. 114) to see the relationships between these

units. The standard unit for the metric system is the liter, which is a little more than 4 cups.

10. Give each group a plastic 2-cup measuring container and a 4-cup measuring container in addition to the 1-cup container they already have. Point out to them that one side of the cup has line markings in U.S. customary units. They should use this side for the following exercise.

11. Ask students to measure 1 cup of water using the 1-cup container. Then have them pour the water into the 2-cup container. Repeat. The water level in the 2-cup container should now measure 2 cups, or 1 pint. Have students do this same exercise with the 4-cup container by filling it with 4 cups of water, measuring to 1 quart. Note the change in appearance of one cup in each of the containers. Ask students the following questions:
    a. Does 1 cup of water look the same in each of the graduated cylinders?
    b. Does the volume of water change when you pour it from the 1-cup container to the 2-cup container or the 4-cup container? Why or why not? How do you know?

12. For the next exercise, have each group of students pour ½ cup of water into their 1-cup container. Then, direct their attention to the opposite side of their measuring cup. Point out that this side has line markings that allow for measuring of volume in metric units, or milliliters (abbreviated as ml on the container).

13. Show students how to use the milliliter markings to measure the volume of a liquid. When the water level does not coincide with a milliliter line marking, explain to students that they can estimate the number of milliliters by choosing the line that the water level is closest to. Have students measure the number of milliliters that is equivalent to a ½ cup of water and record the number on the Units of Volume handout.

14. Next, have students measure 1 cup of water and determine its equivalence in millimeters. Have students record their findings on the Units of Volume handout. Repeat this procedure for 2-cup and 4-cup volumes of water. Ask them what they might infer about the volume of liquids in different measuring cups.

15. Read the fable "The Crow and the Pitcher" to students (below).

> A crow, half-dead with thirst, came upon a pitcher which had once been full of water; but when the crow put its beak into the mouth of the pitcher he found that only very little water was left in it, and that he could not reach far enough down to get at it. He tried, and he tried, but at last had to give up in despair. Then a thought came to him, and he took a pebble and dropped it into the pitcher. Then he took another pebble and dropped it into the pitcher. Then he took another pebble and dropped that into the pitcher. Then he took another pebble and dropped that into the pitcher. Then he took another pebble and dropped that into the pitcher. Then he took another pebble and dropped that into the pitcher. At last, at last, he saw the water mount up near him, and after casting in a few more pebbles he was able to quench his thirst and save his life.

Ask students:
    a. How did adding the pebbles change the level of the water? Elicit the response that the pebbles raise the level of the water. Explain the concept that solid objects displace (or take the place of) water.

16. We can use the displacement of water by solid objects to measure the volume of the solid object because we know that the volume of water displaced by the object equals the volume of the object. Demonstrate this to students as follows: Pour colored water into the 1-cup capacity measuring cup to the level of 100 ml of water. (Any easily measured level will work.) Record the volume of the water by itself. Then carefully put the stone in the water without causing water to splash out. How did adding the stone change the water level?

17. Measure the volume of water with the stone in it. Subtract the volume of water without the stone from the volume of water with the stone. This amount represents the volume of the stone. Demonstrate this as necessary.

18. Tell students they are going to conduct an investigation to determine the volume of marbles (or stones). Distribute the Volume Investigation handout (p. 115). Divide students into groups.

19. Provide each group of student with four marbles/stones, a graduated cylinder, and water. Tell students they are going to determine the volume of the four marbles in water. Students should make individual predictions of the volume of the accumulation of each marble when added to water. Have them write their predictions in the hypothesis section of the handout.

20. Tell students to fill their graduated cylinder or measuring cup approximately half full of water. Record how much water is in their cup on the line provided. Ask students if the beginning amount of water makes a difference in their findings.

21. Instruct students to complete the investigation and record the water level after adding each marble. Tell them to be careful not to let any water splash out when adding a new marble. You also may need to help students determine the measurements for the left axis of the graph.

22. After students have completed the investigation, ask them to write their conclusion based on their findings about volume.

23. Concluding Questions/Actions:
    a. What does volume measure?
    b. Can two objects of different shapes have the same volume? How would you design an experiment to find out?
    c. How might you determine the volume of each individual marble in the experiment?
    d. How would you explain what happens when you place a solid object into a liquid?
    e. Do you think that the displacement of water is a manmade or natural change? Justify your answer.
    f. If you wanted to measure a small amount of liquid (less than a cup), which container would be the best to use, a 1-cup container, a 2-cup container, or a 4-cup container? Why?

24. To conclude the lesson, ask students to date and write a new entry in their lab books:
    a. Write a paragraph explaining why it is important for scientists to make accurate measurements.
    b. Draw a picture that explains how you can measure the volume of a liquid and a solid.

Extending the Lesson

What to Do at Home
- Ask if you can help with a recipe that requires you to measure several different liquids. Measure the liquids using the method you learned today in class.

Name:_____ Date:_____

Measuring Volume

Comparing the Volume of Solids

	Volume in Centimeter Cubes	Draw Your Structure
Structure 1		
Structure 2		

Comparing the Volume of Liquids

Color the graduated containers below so that each one shows 1 ½ cups of liquid.

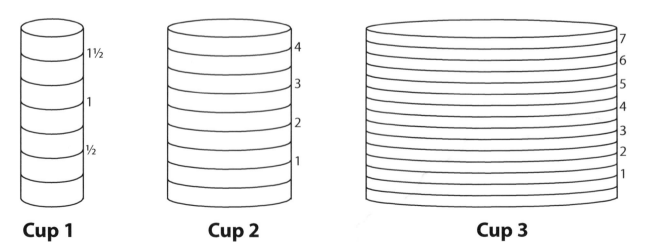

Cup 1   Cup 2   Cup 3

Name:_____ Date:_____

Units of Volume

U.S. Customary Units

2 cups = 1 pint
4 cups = 1 quart
16 cups = 1 gallon

Metric Units

1000 milliliters = 1 liter

Comparison of U.S. Customary to Metric Units

Estimate the numbers of milliliters.

½ cup = _____ milliliters

1 cup = _____ milliliters

2 cups = _____ milliliters

Name:_____ Date:_____

Volume Investigation

Question: What is the volume of one, two, three, and four marbles?

Hypothesis:

One marble _____   Two marbles _____

Three marbles_____   Four marbles _____

My data:

Volume before I placed marbles in the water: _____

Use the graph below to record the water volume after adding each marble.

Volume	**Marble 1**	**Marble 2**	**Marble 3**	**Marble 4**

My conclusion:

_____

_____

_____

_____

_____

Lesson 12:
Evaporation Findings

Planning the Lesson

Instructional Purposes: To understand evaporation and draw conclusions about their findings from the principal's ocean water; to continue work on an independent investigation.

Instructional Time: 45 minutes

Essential Science Understandings:
- Matter is anything that has mass and takes up space.
- Matter can change from one state to another; these changes are referred to as physical changes.
- Temperature and energy can create physical changes in matter.
- Materials are composed of parts that are too small to see without magnification.

Scientific Investigation Skills and Processes:
- Create meaning from the experiment.
- Tell others what was found.

Change Concept Generalizations:
- Change is everywhere.
- Change is linked to time.
- Change can be random or predictable.
- Change can be natural or manmade.

What to Look for in Assessment:
- Are students able to draw appropriate conclusions based on data?
- Are students able to able to explain what happens during evaporation?
- Are students able to begin planning their own investigation?

Materials/Resources/Equipment:
- Student data sheets from the evaporation lesson
- Results from the Ocean Water Data Log (p. 93)
- Word wall card: evaporation
- Student lab books

Implement the Lesson

1. Instruct students to get their lab sheets from the ocean water experiment. Ask students to share their results. Ask:
   a. What do you think happened to the water in the dish? Why?
   b. What factors contributed to the water disappearing?

c. How might you explain what happened in scientific terms? (e.g., what do you know about molecules and temperature that might help you explain to the principal what happened?)
d. What additional questions do you have based on this experiment?

2. Review with students that matter can go from a liquid to a solid and back to a liquid again through the process of freezing and melting. The melting point is the temperature at which a solid begins to change to a liquid. The freezing point is the temperature at which a liquid begins to change to a solid. Remind them that the particles of gas have more energy than the particles of a liquid or solid. They also should be reminded that heating matter adds energy to the particles and makes them speed up and move farther apart.
a. What do they think will happen when energy, in the form of heat, is added to a liquid? (It turns into a gas.)

3. Ask students if they have ever watched what happens when an adult has heated a pot of water on the stove. Elicit the response that when the water gets very hot, it begins to boil. Tell them that this is not something that they should try themselves at home because boiling water can cause serious burns!
a. After the water begins to boil, what happens? (Elicit the response that the water turns into water vapor, the gas form of water. If the water boils long enough, all of it will turn into water vapor and disappear.)

4. The temperature at which a particular type of liquid begins to boil is called its *boiling point*. This temperature is different for different kinds of liquids. For example, the boiling point of water is different from the boiling point of vinegar, which is different from the boiling point of oil.

5. Introduce the concept of evaporation to students. Adding heat to a liquid until it reaches its boiling point causes all of the particles in the liquid to move fast enough to turn into gas. Even when a liquid has not been heated to the boiling point, however, the molecules on the surface of the liquid that are in contact with air can escape into the air and turn into gas. This process is called *evaporation*. Ask students where they think the water goes. (Into the air.) Tell them that the sun makes water evaporate because it supplies heat to the liquid water. Water also will evaporate in the shade or indoors, but at a slower rate. Ask students:
a. Why do you think water will evaporate more slowly if it is in the shade or inside than if it is in the sun?

In summary, there are two ways that a liquid can turn into a gas. When a liquid is heated to its boiling point, it turns into a gas through boiling. When the liquid is cooler than the boiling point, however, liquid at the surface can change into gas through evaporation.

6. Ask students how this new information applies to their observations with the water and salt.
a. What happened to the water? The salt? (Water evaporated; salt did not.)
b. Why did the water evaporate?
c. Would the principal's ocean water evaporate if his or her office was not hot? Why or why not?
d. Does the degree of the temperature matter in the rate of evaporation? Why or why not? How could you conduct an investigation to find out?
e. Do all liquids evaporate? How could you conduct an experiment to find out?

  f. Explain changes over time in this investigation. Do other change generalizations apply?

7. Invite the principal back to the classroom so the students may explain what happened to his or her ocean water (or ask students to write a letter to the principal in their lab books).

8. Allow students time to work on their individual experiments for the Matter Conference. Meet with students as necessary. By this time students should be have the steps of their investigation in place and should be seeking approval to begin experimentation.

9. Concluding Questions/Actions:

  a. Knowing what you know about evaporation of water, when do you think it would be better to water your outdoor plants, at noon or at 6 p.m.? Why? (You should water the plants at 6 p.m. because less water will evaporate than at noon, when the sun is hotter.)

  b. How are boiling and evaporation alike? How are they different?

  c. You have learned that change is everywhere. List as many examples as you can think of places where evaporation takes place. (Evaporation of water from lakes or rivers, evaporation of sweat from skin, evaporation of rain that has fallen on a driveway or deck are some examples.)

  d. Provide students with a copy of the master concept map for this unit and ask them to color in the connections they have learned and understand.

10. To conclude the lesson, ask students to date and write a new entry in their lab books:

  a. Write a letter to the principal to tell him your findings. Include your data table as evidence.

Extending the Lesson

What to Do at Home

- At home, design an experiment to test how evaporation of water by the sun works. Conduct your experiment and report the results to your classmates.

Lesson 13:
Condensation

Planning the Lesson

Instructional Purposes: To investigate condensation by examining ice in a bag; to continue work on the independent investigation.

Instructional Time: 45 minutes

Essential Science Understandings:
- Matter is anything that has mass and takes up space.
- Matter can change from one state to another; these changes are referred to as physical changes.
- Temperature and energy can create physical changes in matter.
- Materials are composed of parts that are too small to see without magnification.

Scientific Investigation Skills and Processes:
- Make observations.
- Ask questions.
- Learn more.
- Design an experiment.

Change Concept Generalizations:
- Change is everywhere.
- Change is linked to time.

What to Look for in Assessment:
- Are students able to understand that the water collecting on the outside of the icy bag is coming from the water vapor in the air?

Materials/Resources/Equipment:
- Plastic bag filled with ice for each student or group of students
- Food coloring
- Word wall card: condensation
- Transparency of the Condensation Word Study (p. 122)
- Student lab books

Implementing the Lesson

1. Explain that students have learned that water can turn into water vapor through boiling or evaporation. This process also can happen in reverse. The gas form of water (water vapor) also can turn into liquid water. This is called *condensation*. Water vapor from the air forms liquid droplets when this process happens. We have learned that adding heat energy causes particles of a liquid to speed up and for matter to change to a gas state. When matter changes from a gas to a liquid,

the particles need to slow down and move closer together. Heat energy needs to be removed through the process of cooling.

2. Give each student a baggie with fresh ice in it. Ask them to observe what is happening. They should notice that the outside of the bag begins to steam and then get liquid droplets on it. After about 3 minutes or when liquid begins to form on the outside of the bag, ask students:
    a. Where do you think the water on the outside of the bag comes from? (It comes from water vapor in the air.)

3. Show students that the water comes from the air rather than from the water in the bag by placing a drop of food color in the bag of ice. Then place a paper towel into the colored water. The paper towel will turn the same color as the water. Then wipe the outside surface of the bag with a second paper towel. The second paper towel will be wet, but clear, demonstrating that the water did not come from inside the bag. Ask students the following questions:
    a. Why does the water form on the outside of the bag? (Because the water vapor in the air that comes into contact with the cold surface of the baggie condenses into liquid water.)
    b. What would happen if the ice melts and becomes the same temperature as the room? Would beads of water still remain on the outside of the bag? (Students should be able to explain that once the heat is removed from the ice the energy is gone and the water vapor will no longer collect.)

4. Finally, ask students what they predict might happen when steam or water vapor from the air is cooled. Can gas change states? Ask students if they have ever seen their parents place a lid on a pan that was boiling. What happens? What happens when the lid is removed? Where does the water vapor go?

5. Show the Condensation Word Study (p. 122) on the overhead. Ask students the following question and write the appropriate responses around the outside of the graphic like a web:
    a. How does the definition of the word *condense* explain what happened in our demonstration today?

6. Ask the following questions:
    a. What happens to the particles of a substance when it goes from a liquid to a gas? What happens to the particles when it goes from a gas to a liquid?
    b. One of the change generalizations that we studied is how change relates to time. Based on the ocean water and bag experiments with evaporation and condensation, explain how time is related to changes in the physical state of a substance.
    c. How might you design an experiment to find out if the boiling point of liquids or the melting point of solids is the same or different?

7. Allow students time to work on their experiments for the Matter Conference. Meet with various groups or individuals as necessary to ensure that the students are following the scientific process. Provide students with ideas if they haven't decided on an investigation. Make sure students have all the materials necessary. Most of the experiments should be completed during class time. Give students a deadline for when they must have their experiments and posters completed. Explain that the next lesson will be a practice run-through of the Matter Conference.

8. Determine the date of the Matter Conference and decide who will be invited. Make invitations and send them out. Ask students if there is a way you could incorporate

a solid, liquid, and gas as part of the conference (e.g., balloons as decorations, cookies and juice as refreshments).

9. To conclude the lesson, ask students to date and write a new entry in their investigation lab books:

    a. How are condensation and freezing alike? How are they different? Draw a Venn diagram to show your response. Share with the class.

Extending the Lesson

What to Do at Home

*   Try this activity at home (with supervision) to find out what happens when water vapor or gas cools: Ask a parent to boil a pan of water. Once the water is boiling, take a metal tray or cookie sheet and hold it over the top of the pan of boiling water. What happens? What happens if you place ice cubes on top of the metal tray while holding the pan? Is there a difference? Explain your findings to your parents using scientific vocabulary.

Name:_____ Date:_____

Condensation Word Study

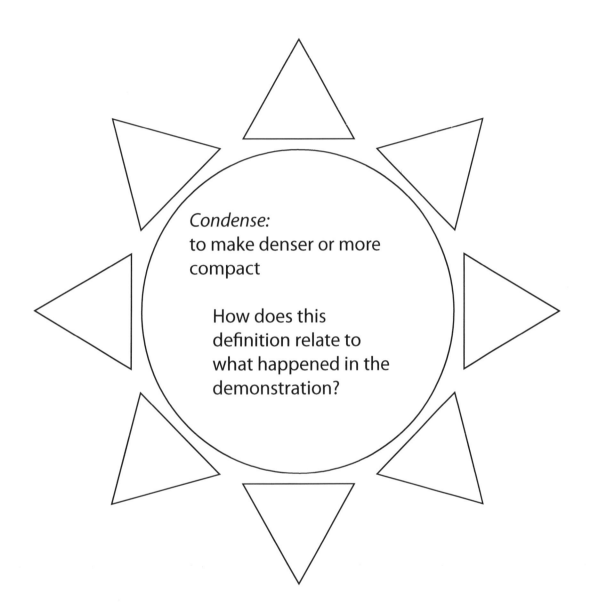

Condense:
to make denser or more compact

How does this definition relate to what happened in the demonstration?

Lesson 14:
Planning the Investigation
and Hosting the Matter Conference

Planning the Lesson

Instructional Purpose: To practice, prepare, and conduct the Matter Conference.

Instructional Time: 45 minutes

Essential Science Understandings:
- All common substances are made of matter.
- Matter is anything that has mass and takes up space.
- There are three states of matter: solids, liquids, and gases.
- Objects can be described by color, shape, texture, relative size and weight, and position.
- Matter can change from one state to another; these changes are referred to as physical changes.
- Volume is the measure of the amount of space occupied by matter.
- Mass is a measure of the amount of matter.
- Materials are composed of parts that are too small to see without magnification.
- Physical properties remain the same when a material is reduced in size.
- Some liquids separate when mixed with water.
- Some solids will dissolve in water, and some dissolve more quickly in hot than cold water.
- Temperature and energy can create physical changes in matter.

Scientific Investigation Skills and Processes:
- Make observations.
- Ask questions.
- Learn more.
- Design and conduct experiments.
- Create meaning from the experiment.
- Tell others what was found.

Change Concept Generalizations:
- Change is everywhere.
- Change is related to time.
- Change can be natural or manmade.
- Change can be random or predictable.

What to Look for in Assessment:
- Have students completed or will complete their investigations?
- Are students able to demonstrate and articulate their findings?
- Are students prepared for the conference?

Materials/Resources/Equipment:
- Student lab books
- Supplies as needed for each group of students or individuals to present their findings from their personal investigations about matter

Implementing the Lesson

1. Ensure that each group of students is prepared to share its findings at the Matter Conference.
2. Allow students the time to complete their investigations, make posters or presentations, and/or practice what they are going to say and do for the Matter Conference.
3. Ask students to examine the word wall. Tell them to make sure they are using words from the word wall as necessary to explain their findings.
4. Determine the format for the Matter Conference. Examples are as follows:
    a. *Option A:* Students set up centers on their desk like a science fair and invitees walk through, observe, and ask questions.
    b. *Option B:* Students are given 2–3 minutes to share their findings with the entire group.
    c. *Option C:* The teacher or select students provide an overview of matter and the scientific process to the group of invitees (no more than 5–10 minutes) and then the invitees walk around and view the student products, as Option A suggests.

5. Host a practice run-through of the Matter Conference so that students will have a firm understanding of what will transpire.
6. Host the Matter Conference immediately after the practice run-through or the next day.
7. To conclude the lesson, ask students to date and write a new entry in their lab books. Share responses in a classroom discussion if time permits. Students should complete the following prompt:
    a. My experiment is important to the Matter Conference because . . .

Extending the Lesson

What to Do at Home
- Share your investigations and other student's investigations about matter with your family. Try replicating one of the experiments from another group at home. Did you find similar or different results? Why is it important for scientists to repeat experiments?

Lesson 15:
Concluding the Unit

Planning the Lesson

Instructional Purpose: To review the unit's science, process, and concept understandings.

Instructional Time: 45 minutes

Essential Science Understandings:
- All common substances are made of matter.
- Matter is anything that has mass and takes up space.
- There are three states of matter: solids, liquids, and gases.
- Objects can be described by color, shape, texture, relative size and weight, and position.
- Matter can change from one state to another; these changes are referred to as physical changes.
- Volume is the measure of the amount of space occupied by matter.
- Mass is a measure of the amount of matter.
- Materials are composed of parts that are too small to see without magnification.
- Physical properties remain the same when a material is reduced in size.
- Some liquids separate when mixed with water.
- Some solids will dissolve in water, and some dissolve more quickly in hot than cold water.
- Temperature and energy can create physical changes in matter.

Scientific Investigation Skills and Processes:
- Make observations.
- Ask questions.
- Learn more.
- Design and conduct experiments.
- Create meaning from the experiment.
- Tell others what was found.

Change Concept Generalizations:
- Change is everywhere.
- Change is related to time.
- Change can be natural or manmade.
- Change can be random or predictable.

What to Look for in Assessment:
- Are students able to explain what they have learned throughout the unit?
- Are students able to provide examples of changes?

Materials/Resources/Equipment:
- Index cards with words from the word wall written on them

- Copies of Examples of Change Cutouts and Examples of Change Chart (pp. 128–129) for each student
- Stickers or badges for each student made from page 130
- Student lab books

Implementing the Lesson

1. Ask students to reflect on the Matter Conference in a classroom discussion. What did they like? What did they learn? What would they do differently next time?
2. Tell students that in this lesson you are going to review everything they've learned over the past few weeks while studying matter.
3. Divide students into six groups. Give each group a set of index cards with concept words from the word wall as follows (one word per index card):
   a. *Group One*: scientific process, observation, experiment, hypothesis, conclusion
   b. *Group Two*: solids, liquids, gases, molecules, physical changes
   c. *Group Three*: melting point, freezing point, molecules, physical changes
   d. *Group Four*: matter, mass, volume, solids, liquids, displacement
   e. *Group Five*: evaporation, condensation, water vapor, molecules, dissolve
   f. *Group Six*: solids, liquids, gases, properties, states, matter, change

4. Tell students that they must design a way to use all of the words you gave them and demonstrate for the class how the words fit together. They may do this in the form of a concept map, a skit, a poster, or any other demonstration with your approval. Explain to students that they have 15 minutes to figure out what to do and 1 minute to share their demonstration with the class. Set the timer and monitor each group, reminding them when they have 5 minutes left. (Tell students they may use additional words if necessary, but they must use all of the words you gave them.)
5. Allow time for each group to share its findings. Clarify any misconceptions as necessary.
6. Tell students that you have been discussing change during the unit. Ask them what they've learned about changes in matter. Write their responses on the board.
7. Distribute Examples of Change Cutouts (p. 128) and Examples of Change Chart (p. 129). With a partner, instruct students to cut the strips from page 128 and place them in the appropriate boxes on p. 129. Emphasize that some examples may fit more than one change generalization.
8. Review the finalized Examples of Change Chart, asking students to justify their answers.
9. Proclaim that students have completed the unit on matter and have become great scientists. Give students a badge to celebrate their completion of the matter unit using the matter badges on p. 130. You may choose to call up each student individually and allow all of the students to applaud.
10. Concluding Questions/Actions:
    a. Ask students to work with a partner to make a concept map of what they have learned in this unit. Give them a topic word to begin or a question to respond to in concept map form.

11. To conclude the lesson, ask students to date and write a new entry in their lab books. Share responses in a classroom discussion if time permits. Students should complete the following prompts:
    a. My favorite part of studying matter was . . .

b.   The most important thing that I learned is . . .

Extending the Lesson

What to Do at Home
- Continue to act like a scientist. Go to the library and check out books on matter or another topic you are interested in. Read and learn more. Conduct experiments with your family.

Examples of Change Cutouts

Cut out the boxes below and attach the cutouts in the relating boxes on the Examples of Change Chart. Or, write the following phrases in the appropriate box on the chart.

Ocean water experiment (evaporation)	Mass of a solid or liquid does not change when the matter goes through a physical change
Condensation on the outside of a bag of ice	The volume of liquids
Molecules that speed up or slow down depending on the temperature	The physical property of an object does not change when the size is reduced or enlarged
Matter is anything that has mass and takes up space	Temperature and energy can create physical changes in matter
Matter can change from one state to another; these changes are referred to as physical changes	Mass is a measure of the amount of matter
Materials are composed of parts that are too small to see without magnification	There are three states of matter: solids, liquids, and gases
All common substances are made of matter	Making ice cream
Physical changes in matter	Chemical changes in matter
Being a scientist	Oil and water experiment
Balloon in the bottle demonstration	Ice cube changing to water
The mystery goop (suspensions)	Water freezing and changing to an ice cube
Freezing	Water changing to water vapor
Melting	The investigation I did for the Matter Conference
Solids dissolve more quickly in hot water than cold water	Some liquids separate when mixed with water

Name:_____ Date:_____

Examples of Change Chart

Change Generalizations	Examples
Change is linked to time.	
Change can be manmade or natural.	
Change can be random or predictable.	
Change is everywhere.	

Matter Badges

I Know
About Matter!
Ask Me About It!

I Know
About Matter!
Ask Me About It!

I Know
About Matter!
Ask Me About It!

I Know
About Matter!
Ask Me About It!

I Know
About Matter!
Ask Me About It!

Postassessment

Planning the Postassessment

Instructional Purpose: To assess student knowledge of unit content.

Instructional Time:
- Concept assessment: 30 minutes
- Scientific process assessment: 20 minutes
- Content assessment: 30 minutes

Materials/Resources/Equipment Needed:
- Copies of postassessments for unit concept, process, and content
- Pencils

Activities:
- Give each student a copy of the postassessments to complete in the order noted above. The assessments should take no more than 80 minutes in all. Explain that the assessment will be used to see how much students have learned during the unit.

Scoring:
- Use rubrics to evaluate concept, scientific process, and content postassessment results.

Name:_____ Date:_____

Postassessment for Change Concept

1. Give as many examples of things that change as you can, up to 10.

- _____
- _____
- _____
- _____
- _____
- _____
- _____
- _____
- _____
- _____

2. Draw one example of something that changes, showing before and after the change. Provide as many details as you can.

Before	After

3. Identify five ways that a tree could change or be changed.

- _____
- _____
- _____
- _____
- _____

4. What are *three* things you can say about all change?

All change

_____
_____
_____

All change

_____
_____
_____

All change

_____
_____
_____

Name: _____ Date: _____

Postassessment for Change Concept: Grading Rubric

		5	4	3	2	1	0
1	**Examples of the Concept**	At least 9–10 appropriate examples are given.	At least 7–8 appropriate examples are given.	At least 5–6 appropriate examples are given.	At least 3 appropriate examples are given.	At least 1–2 appropriate examples are given.	No examples are given.
2	**Drawing of Before–After**	The drawing contains at least five changed elements depicting a before–after situation.	The drawing contains four changed elements depicting a before–after situation.	The drawing contains three changed elements that depict a before–after situation.	The drawing contains two elements and does not clearly indicate a change relationship.	The drawing contains only one picture element or does not show a before–after relationship.	The drawing contains no elements.
3	**Types of Change**	Five different types of changes are identified.	Four different types of changes are identified.	Three different types of changes are identified.	Two different types of changes are identified.	One different type of change is identified.	No type of change is identified.
4	**Generalizations**	Reflects three appropriate generalizations about change.	Reflects three somewhat appropriate generalizations about change.	Reflects two appropriate generalizations about change.	Reflects one appropriate generalization about change.	Reflects only a statement about change.	No statements or generalizations about change are provided.

Total Points: _____ / 20

Name:_____ Date:_____

Postassessment for Scientific Process

1. How would you study the following question: Are plants attracted to the sun?

   _____

   _____

   _____

   _____

   _____

2. Describe an experiment to test this question that includes the following:

   a. Make a prediction regarding the question: Are plants attracted to the sun?

   I predict that

   _____

   _____

   _____

   _____

   b. What materials will be needed to conduct the experiment?

   _____

   _____

   _____

   _____

   _____

c. What steps must be taken to conduct the experiment and in what order?

_____

_____

_____

_____

_____

d. What data do you want to collect and how should it be recorded?

_____

_____

_____

_____

e. How do the data help you decide if your prediction is correct? Explain.

_____

_____

_____

_____

Name:_____ Date:_____

Postassessment for Scientific Process: Grading Rubric

Criteria	Strong Evidence 3	Some Evidence 2	Little Evidence 1	No Evidence 0
2a. Generates a prediction.	Clearly generates a prediction appropriate to the experiment.	Somewhat generates a prediction appropriate to the experiment.	Generates an inappropriate prediction.	Fails to generate a prediction.
2b. Lists materials needed.	Provides an inclusive and appropriate list of materials. Provides a list of 5–6 materials.	Provides a partial list of appropriate materials needed. Provides a list of 3–4 materials.	Provides inappropriate materials. OR Provides only 1–2 appropriate materials.	Fails to provide a list of materials needed.
2c. Lists experiment steps.	Clearly and concisely lists 4 or more steps as appropriate for the experiment design.	Clearly and concisely lists 2–3 steps as appropriate for the experiment design.	Generates at least 1 appropriate step.	Fails to generate experiment steps.
2c. Arranges steps in sequential order.	N/A	Lists experiment steps in sequential order.	Lists 2 or fewer experiment steps or places them in an illogical order.	Does not list steps.
2d. Plans data collection.	Clearly states a plan for data collection, including what data will be needed and how they will be recorded.	States a partial plan for data collection, citing some items for collection and some way of recording data.	Provides an incomplete plan for either data collection or recording.	Fails to identify any part of a plan for data collection.
2e. States plan for interpreting data for making predictions.	Clearly states plan for interpreting data by linking data to prediction.	States a partial plan for interpreting data that links data to prediction.	Provides a brief statement that partially addresses use of data for prediction.	Fails to state plan for using data for making a prediction.

Total Score: _____ / 17

Note. Adapted from Fowler, M. (1990). The diet cola test. *Science Scope, 13,* 32–34.

Postassessment for Content: Teacher Directions

Read the following paragraph to students.

Today I would like for you to think about all of the things you know about matter. Think about the words you would use and the pictures you could draw to make a concept map. Think about the connections you can make. On your own paper, draw in pictures and words that you know about matter. You will be drawing a concept map, just like the ones you did when we discussed the farm at the beginning of this unit. The subject of your concept map is: "Tell me everything you know about matter."

Have students draw a concept map for matter on their own paper.

Name:_____ Date:_____

Postassessment for Content: Grading Rubric

		5	4	3	2	1	0
1	**Hierarchical Level** *Each subordinate concept is more specific and less general than the concept drawn above it. Count the number of levels included in the total map.*	Five or more levels are identified.	Four levels are identified.	Three levels are identified	Two levels are identified.	One level is identified.	No hierarchical levels are identified.
2	**Propositions** *The linking of two concepts indicating a clear relationship is given. Count the total number of propositions identified on the total map.*	Student provides more than 12 propositions.	Student provides 10–12 propositions.	Student provides 7–9 propositions.	Student provides 4–6 propositions.	Student provides 1–3 propositions.	Student provides no propositions.
3	**Examples** *A valid example of a concept is provided. Count the total number of examples on the total map.*	Student provides more than 12 examples.	Student provides 10–12 examples.	Student provides 7–9 examples.	Student provides 4–6 examples.	Student provides 1–3 examples.	Student provides no examples.

Total Points: _____ / 15

Appendix A: Teaching Models

Several teaching models are incorporated into the Project Clarion units. These models ensure emphasis on unit outcomes and support student understanding of the concepts and processes that are the focus of each unit. Teachers should become familiar with these models and how to use them before teaching the unit. The first three models are used in every Project Clarion unit. The last model is used as appropriate to the outcomes of the specific units. The models are listed below and outlined in the pages that follow.

1. The Taba Model of Concept Development
2. The Wheel of Scientific Investigation and Reasoning
3. Concept Mapping
4. The Frayer Model of Vocabulary Development

The Taba Model of Concept Development

Each Project Clarion unit supports the development of a specific overarching concept (change, systems, or cause and effect). The concept development model, based upon the work of Hilda Taba (1962), supports student learning of the overarching concept. The model involves both inductive and deductive reasoning processes and focuses on the creation of generalizations about the overarching concept from a student-derived list of created concept examples. The model includes a series of steps, with each step involving student participation. Students begin with a broad concept, determine specific examples from that broad concept, create appropriate categorization systems, cite nonexamples of the concept, establish generalizations based on their understanding, and then apply the generalizations to their readings and other situations.

The model generally is most effective when small groups of students work through each step, with whole-class debriefing following each stage of the process. However, with primary-age students, additional teacher guidance may be necessary, especially for the later stages of the model. The steps of the model are outlined below, using the unit concept of change.

1. Students generate examples of the concept of change, derived from their own understanding and experiences with change in the world. Teachers should encourage students to provide at least 15–20 examples; a class list may be created out of the small-group lists to lengthen the set of changes students have to work with.

2. Students then group their changes into categories. This process allows students to search for interrelatedness and to organize their thinking. It often is helpful to have individual examples written on cards so that the categorization may occur physically, as well as mentally or in writing. Students then should explain their reasoning for their categorization system and seek clarification from each other as a whole group. Teachers should ensure that all examples have been accounted for in the categorization system established.

3. Students then generate a list of nonexamples of the concept of change. Teachers may begin this step with the direction, "Now list examples of things that *do not change.*" Encourage students to think carefully about their nonexamples and discuss ideas within their groups. Each group should list five to six nonexamples.

4. The students next determine generalizations about the concept of change, using their lists of examples, categories, and nonexamples. Teachers then should share the unit generalizations and relate valid student generalizations to the unit list. Both lists should be posted in the room throughout the course of the unit.
5. During the unit, students are asked to identify specific examples of the generalizations from their own readings, or to describe how the concept applies to a given situation about which they have read. Students also are asked to apply the generalizations to their own writings and their own lives. Several lessons employ a chart that lists several of the generalizations and asks students to supply examples specifically related to the reading or activity of that lesson.

The Wheel of Scientific Investigation and Reasoning

All scientists work to improve our knowledge and understanding of the world. In the process of scientific inquiry, scientists connect evidence with logical reasoning. Scientists also apply their imagination as they devise hypotheses and explanations that make sense of the evidence. Students can strengthen their understanding of particular science topics through investigations that cause them to employ evidence gathering, logical reasoning, and creativity. The Wheel of Scientific Investigation and Reasoning contains the specific processes involved in scientific inquiry to guide students' thinking and actions.

Make Observations

Scientists make careful observation and try things out. They must describe things as accurately as possible so that they can compare their observations from one time to another and so that they can compare their observations with those of other scientists. Scientists use their observations to form questions for investigation.

Ask Questions

Scientific investigations usually are initiated through a problem to be solved or a question to be asked. Selecting just the right question or clearly defining the problem to be addressed is critical to the investigation process.

Learn More

To clarify their questions, scientists learn more by reviewing bodies of scientific knowledge documented in text and in previously conducted investigations. Also, when scientists get conflicting information from the information they have gathered, they make fresh observations and insights that may result in revision of the previously formed question. By learning more, scientists can design and conduct more effective experiments or build upon previously conducted experiments.

Design and Conduct the Experiment

Scientists use their collection of relevant evidence, their reasoning, and their imagination to develop a hypothesis. Sometimes scientists have more than one possible explanation for the same set of observations and evidence. Often when additional observations and testing are completed, scientists modify current scientific knowledge.

To test out hypotheses, scientists design experiments that will enable them to control conditions so that their results will be reliable. Scientists always repeat their experiment, doing it the same way it was done before and expecting to get very similar although not exact results. It is important to control conditions in order to make comparisons. Scientists sometimes are not sure what will happen because they don't know everything that might be having an effect on their experiment.

Create Meaning From the Experiment

Scientists analyze the data that are collected from the experiment to add to the existing body of scientific knowledge. They organize their data using data tables and graphs and then make inferences from the data to draw conclusions about whether their question was answered and the effectiveness of their experiments. Scientists also create meaning by comparing what they found to existing knowledge. The analysis of experiment data and process often leads to identification of related questions and future experiments.

Tell Others What Was Found

In the investigation process, scientists often work as a team, sharing findings with each other so that they may benefit from the results. Initially individual team members complete their own work and draw their own conclusions.

One way to introduce the wheel to students is to provide them with the graphic model and ask them to tell one reason why each section of the wheel is important to scientific investigation. The end of this appendix (pp. 149–151) includes several handouts that can be used with students to teach The Wheel of Scientific Investigation and Reasoning.

Concept Mapping

Overview

A concept map is a graphic representation of one's knowledge on a particular topic. Concept maps support learning, teaching, and evaluation (Novak & Gowin, 1984). Students clarify and extend their own thinking about a topic. Teachers find concept mapping useful for envisioning the scope of a lesson or unit. They also use student-developed concept maps as a way of measuring their progress. Meaningful concept maps often begin with a particular question (focus question) about a topic, event, or object.

Concept maps were developed in 1972 as part of research conducted by Dr. Joseph Novak at Cornell University. Dr. Novak was working with young children's understanding of science concepts. Students were interviewed by researchers who recorded their responses. The researchers sought an effective way to identify changes in students' understanding over time. Analysis of transcripts of students' verbal responses proved to be very difficult. Basing their work on Ausubel's cognitive psychology, Novak and his research colleagues began to represent the students' conceptual understanding in concept maps. Ausubel's cognitive psychology supports the idea that learning takes place through the assimilation of new concepts and propositions into existing concept and propositional frameworks.

As seen in Figure 6, concept maps show concepts and relationships between them. The concepts are contained within boxes or oval shapes, and the connections between concepts are represented by lines with linking words.

Concepts are the students' perceived ideas generalized from particular experiences. Sometimes the concepts placed on the map may contain more than one word. Words placed on the line are linking words or phrases and the labels for the words that contain propositions. The propositions contain two or more concepts connected by linking words or phrases to form a meaningful statement.

The youngest students may view and develop concept maps making basic connections. They may begin with two concepts joined by a linking word. These

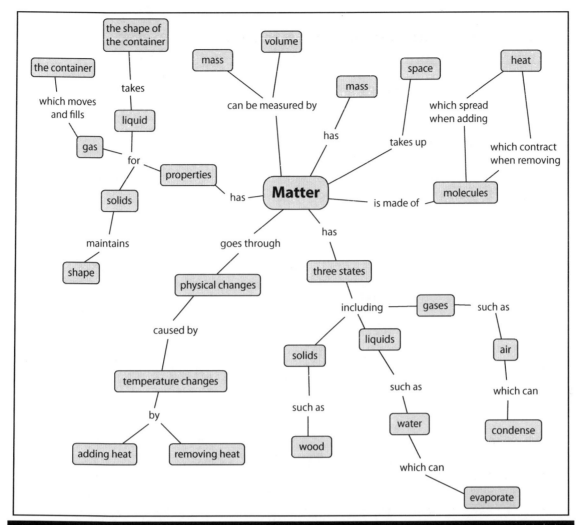

Figure 6. A concept map showing a student's understanding of matter.

"sentences" (propositions) become the building blocks for concept maps. Older students may begin to make multiple connections immediately as they develop their maps.

As students map their knowledge base, they begin to represent their conceptual understanding in a hierarchical manner. The broadest, most inclusive concepts often are found at the top of a concept map. More specific concepts and examples then follow.

Each Project Clarion unit contains an overview concept map, showing the essential knowledge included in the lessons and the connections students should be able to make as a result of their experiences within the unit. This overview may be useful as a classroom poster that the teacher and students may refer to throughout the unit.

Strategies to Prepare for Concept Mapping

The following strategies (adapted from Novak & Gowin, 1984) will help you prepare your students for the concept mapping activities.

What Do Words Mean?
1. Ask students to picture in their minds some common words (water, tree, door, box, pencil, dog). Start with "object words," saying them one at a time, allowing time for students to picture each of them.
2. Create a class list of object words, asking students to name other objects they can picture in their minds to add to the list.

3. Next create a list of "event" words such as jumping, running, or eating. Ask students to envision each of these in their minds and encourage them to contribute to the class list of event words.

4. Give students a few words that are likely to be unfamiliar to most of them, asking if they can see a picture in their mind. Words should be short, such as data, cell, prey, or inertia. You might include a few simple words in another language. Ask students if they have any mind pictures.

5. Discuss the fact that words are useful to us because they convey meaning. This only happens when they can form a picture in their mind that represents the meaning they connect with the word.

What Is a Concept?

1. Introduce the word *concept* and explain that concept is the word we use to mean some kind of object or event we can picture in our mind. Refer back to the word lists previously developed as you discuss the word and ask if these are concepts. Can they see a picture in their mind for each of them? Let students know that when they come upon a word they do not know well enough to form a picture, they will just need to learn the concept associated with that new word. Learning new concepts is exciting and they will learn new ones in their science unit.

2. Provide each table with a few picture cards and ask students to take turns at their table naming some of the concepts included in the card.

What Are Linking Words?

1. Prepare a list of words such as the, is, are, when, that, and then. Ask students if they can see a picture in their mind for each of these words. Explain that these are not concept words. These are linking words we use when we speak or write to link concept words together into sentences that have special meaning. Ask students if they have any words to add to the list. Label the list *Linking Words*.

2. Hold up two picture cards (sky and blue) and give students a sample sentence ("The sky is blue.") Ask students to tell you the concept words and the linking words in your sentence. Give another example.

3. Give each pair of students a few picture cards. Ask the students to work with partners to pick up two cards and then develop a sentence that links the two cards. They should take turns, with one partner making the sentence and the other identifying the concepts and the linking words. Ask them to repeat this a few times and then have several partners share their sentences.

4. Explain to students that it is easy to make up sentences and to read sentences where the printed labels (words) are familiar to them. Explain that reading and writing sentences is like making a link between two things (concepts) they already know. Practice this idea during reading time, asking students to find a sentence and analyze it for concepts and linking words.

Learning to Build a Concept Map (Novak & Gowin, 1984)

1. Make a list of 12–15 related and familiar concept words. Do not use words from the unit. Organize words from more general, more inclusive concepts to less general, more specific concepts. Here are two sets that work well.
   - city, buildings, streets, people, transportation, noise, elevator, stores, offices, one way, taxis, limousines, subway, workers, tourists. This set can be used in conjunction with the children' book, *Do Skyscrapers Touch the Sky?: First Questions and Answers About the City* by TIME-Life.
   - farm, animals, farmer, cow, horse, crops, soil, corn, potatoes, barn, machinery, tractor, harvest, food

2. Tell students that they are going to participate in an activity that uses their understanding of concepts and linking words. Tell them that they will develop a concept map. First, show a simple concept map (my pet, a school bus) on chart paper or with an electronic device (computer, smart board, overhead projector). Give students one example of a "sentence" contained in the map. Ask them to tell the concept words and the linking words. Then ask students to find another sentence and describe the parts. Ask students if they can think of other links to add to the map. Give partners a copy of the map and ask them to add one or more links to the map.

3. Give partners a list of related words and ask them to play around with them until they have selected two or more to link together. Ask students to paste their words on their papers and write in the linking words.

4. Ask students to make a concept map, using a few words you provide, based on a familiar topic. Allow students to add other words and pictures as they wish. Ask students to share their maps with partners and then share a few with the whole class.

Concept Mapping Practice Activities

1. Provide students with picture cards and ask them to select two things that go together in some way. Students should tell what they selected and then make a sentence about the two objects that show a link.

2. Give partners a set of related picture cards and a topic. Also provide the partners with a piece of yarn. Ask students to work together to decide on a linking sentence. When they have a good link, they should hold up their cards and link themselves together stretching the yarn in their hands.

3. Give students a copy of a very basic concept map with some blank areas. Provide the appropriate responses on paper for students to cut out and add to the map to make it complete.

4. Provide a center activity with a list of linking words and picture cards. Use either general pictures or pictures specific to the unit. Encourage students to practice making mapping sentences by using two cards and connecting them with linking words.

5. Ask students to create their own pictures that show the linking of two concepts.

6. Ask students to select three concept pictures and link them together.

7. Ask students to create pictures that show the linking of three concepts they have selected from the set of concept cards.

8. Given a set of related words, ask students to develop a concept map on the table, using the cards and then adding linking words on small blank cards.

9. Given a set of related words, ask students to develop a concept map on paper, either gluing the cards onto a large sheet or drawing the objects and adding the linking words.

10. Ask students a question about a particular topic and ask them to use a bank of words and or pictures to create a concept map that responds to the question. Encourage students to add words to the bank to use in the map.

Using Concept Mapping in Unit Lessons

Rationale: Practice in using concept maps supports student learning as they begin to build upon known concepts. Students begin to add new concepts to their initial understanding of a topic and to make new connections between concepts. The use of concept maps within the lessons also helps teachers to recognize students' conceptual frameworks so that instruction can be adapted as necessary. Student-developed maps also frequently reveal student misconceptions in science.

Strategies:
1. Provide a large unit concept map as a constant poster on the wall, referring to it at critical times to reinforce new learning.
2. Use some aspect of concept mapping as a warm-up or review of the lesson. You can display a concept map of what is going to be experienced in the lesson or as a review at the end of the lesson.
3. Use concept mapping "sentences" to reinforce new concepts in the lesson, providing students with opportunities to make links with their new knowledge.
4. Encourage students to take home several of the key concept words or pictures for sharing with parents or guardians. Ask students to show their families how they can link two of the concepts.
5. Develop a large concept map for the overarching concept in your unit, referring to the generalizations and asking students to make links to add to the map with sticky notes.

The Frayer Model of Vocabulary Development

The Frayer Model of Vocabulary Development (Frayer, Frederick, & Klausmeier, 1969) provides students with a graphic organizer that asks them to think about and describe the meaning of a word or concept (see Figures 7 and 8 for examples of blank and completed Frayer Model organizers). This process enables them to strengthen their understanding of vocabulary words. Through the model students are required to consider the important characteristics of the word and to provide examples and nonexamples of the concept. This model has similarities to the Taba Concept Development Model.

In introducing the Frayer Model to your students, demonstrate its use on large chart paper. Begin with a word all students know such as rock, umbrella, or shoe, placing it on the graphic model. First, ask the students to define the word in their own words. Record a definition that represents their common knowledge. Next, ask students to give specific characteristics of the word/concept or facts they know about it. Record these ideas. Then ask students to offer examples of the idea and then nonexamples to finish the graphic.

Another way to use the Frayer Model is to provide students with examples and nonexamples and ask them to consider what word or concept is being analyzed. You can provide similar exercises by filling in some portions of the graphic and asking students to complete the remaining sections.

As students share ideas, note the level of understanding of the group and of individual students. As the unit is taught, certain vocabulary words may need this type of expanded thinking to support student readiness for using the vocabulary in the science activities. You may want students to maintain individual notebooks of words so that they can refer back to them in their work.

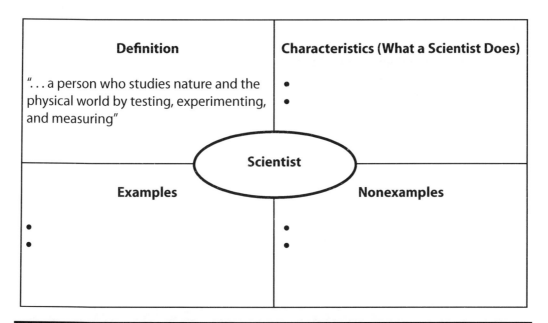

Figure 7. Blank Frayer Model of Vocabulary Development graphic organizer.

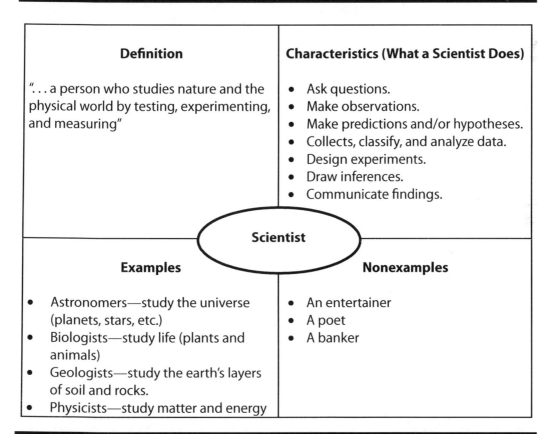

Figure 8. Completed graphic organizer for Frayer Model.

Name:_____ Date:_____

The Wheel of Scientific Investigation and Reasoning

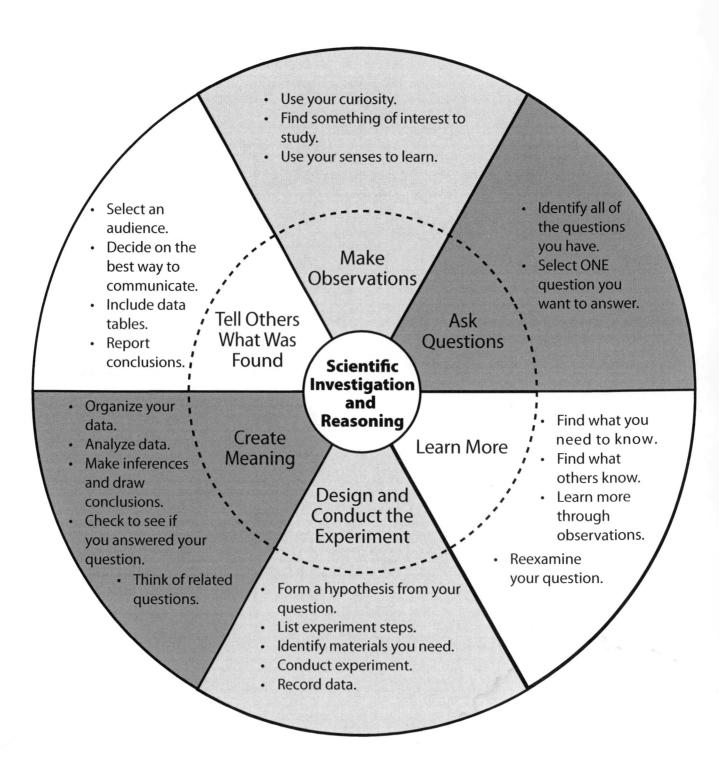

Use your curiosity.
Find something of interest to study.
Use your senses to learn.

Make Observations

Identify all of the questions you have.
Select ONE question you want to answer.

Ask Questions

Select an audience.
Decide on the best way to communicate.
Include data tables.
Report conclusions.

Tell Others What Was Found

Scientific Investigation and Reasoning

Learn More

Find what you need to know.
Find what others know.
Learn more through observations.

Reexamine your question.

Organize your data.
Analyze data.
Make inferences and draw conclusions.
Check to see if you answered your question.
Think of related questions.

Create Meaning

Design and Conduct the Experiment

Form a hypothesis from your question.
List experiment steps.
Identify materials you need.
Conduct experiment.
Record data.

Name:_____ Date:_____

What Scientists Do . . .
The Wheel of Scientific Investigation and Reasoning

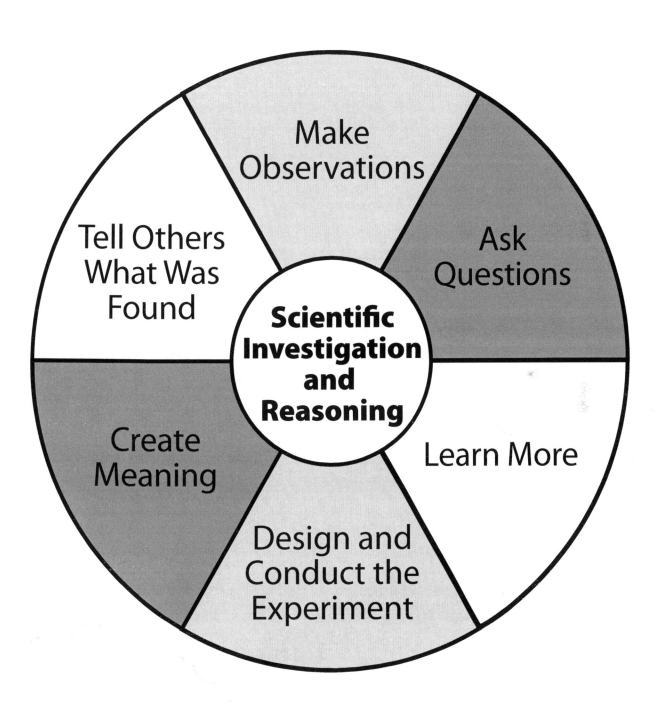

Name:_____ Date:_____

Planning Wheel of Scientific Investigation and Reasoning

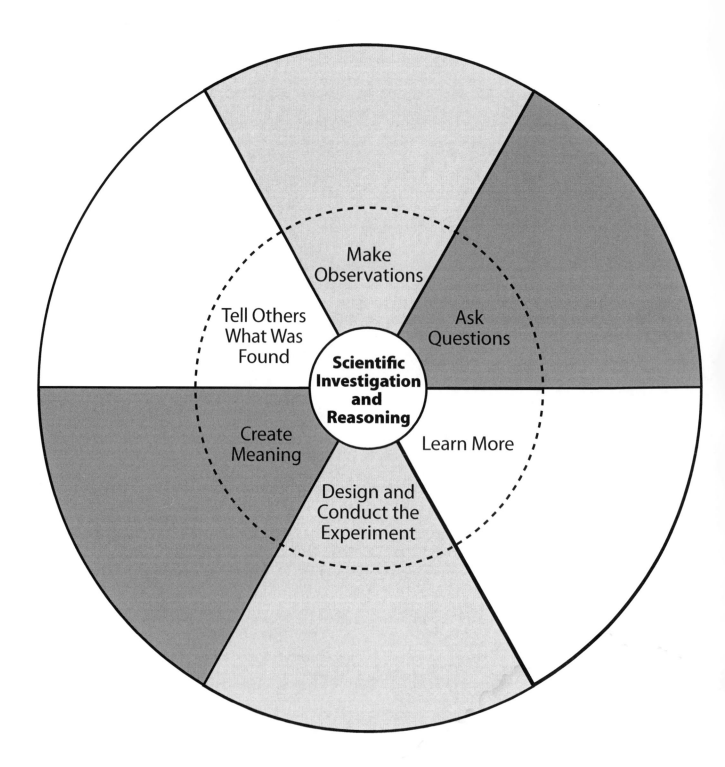

References

Fowler, M. (1990). The diet cola test. *Science Scope, 13,* 32–34.

Frayer, D. A., Frederick, W. C., & Klausmeier, H. J. (1969). *A schema for testing the level of concept mastery* (Technical Report No. 16). Madison: The University of Wisconsin, Wisconsin Research and Development Center for Cognitive Learning.

Judson, H. F. (1980). *The search for solutions.* New York: Holt, Rinehart, and Winston.

Novak, J., & Gowin, B. D. (1984). *Learning how to learn.* New York: Cambridge University Press.

Rutherford, F. J., & Ahlgren, A. (1990). *Science for all Americans: Scientific literacy.* New York: American Association for the Advancement of Science.

Scholastic. (Eds.). (1996). *Scholastic children's dictionary* (Rev. ed.). New York: Author.

Taba, H. (1962). *Curriculum development, theory and practice.* New York: Harcourt Brace.

Common Core State Standards and Next Generation Science Standards Alignment

Lesson	Common Core State Standards and Next Generation Science Standards Met
Lesson 1: What Is Change?	NGSS: 2-PS1-1. Plan and conduct an investigation to describe and classify different kinds of materials by their observable properties.
	CCSS-ELA: SL.2.1 Participate in collaborative conversations with diverse partners about grade 2 topics and texts with peers and adults in small and larger groups.
Lesson 2: What Is a Scientist?	CCSS-ELA: SL.2.1 Participate in collaborative conversations with diverse partners about grade 2 topics and texts with peers and adults in small and larger groups.
	CCSS-ELA: SL.2.2 Recount or describe key ideas or details from a text read aloud or information presented orally or through other media.
Lesson 3: Introduction to Matter	NGSS: 2-PS1-1. Plan and conduct an investigation to describe and classify different kinds of materials by their observable properties.
	CCSS-ELA: SL.2.1 Participate in collaborative conversations with diverse partners about grade 2 topics and texts with peers and adults in small and larger groups.
Lesson 4: What Scientists Do: Observe, Question, Learn More	NGSS: 2-PS1-1. Plan and conduct an investigation to describe and classify different kinds of materials by their observable properties.
	CCSS-ELA: SL.2.1 Participate in collaborative conversations with diverse partners about grade 2 topics and texts with peers and adults in small and larger groups.
Lesson 5: What Scientists Do: Experiment, Create Meaning, Tell Others	NGSS: 2-PS1-1. Plan and conduct an investigation to describe and classify different kinds of materials by their observable properties.
	NGSS: 2-PS1-2. Analyze data obtained from testing different materials to determine which materials have the properties that are best suited for an intended purpose.
	CCSS-ELA: SL.2.1 Participate in collaborative conversations with diverse partners about grade 2 topics and texts with peers and adults in small and larger groups.
Lesson 6: The Case of the Mystery Goop	NGSS: 2-PS1-1. Plan and conduct an investigation to describe and classify different kinds of materials by their observable properties.
	NGSS: 2-PS1-2. Analyze data obtained from testing different materials to determine which materials have the properties that are best suited for an intended purpose.
	CCSS-ELA: SL.2.1 Participate in collaborative conversations with diverse partners about grade 2 topics and texts with peers and adults in small and larger groups.
	CCSS-ELA: L.2.4 Determine or clarify the meaning of unknown and multiple-meaning words and phrases based on grade 2 reading and content, choosing flexibly from an array of strategies.
Lesson 7: Physical Changes by Changing Temperature	NGSS: 2-PS1-1. Plan and conduct an investigation to describe and classify different kinds of materials by their observable properties.
	NGSS: 2-PS1-4. Construct an argument with evidence that some changes caused by heating or cooling can be reversed and some cannot.
	CCSS-ELA: SL.2.1 Participate in collaborative conversations with diverse partners about grade 2 topics and texts with peers and adults in small and larger groups.

Lesson	Common Core State Standards and Next Generation Science Standards Met
Lesson 8: Who Stole the Principal's Water?	NGSS: 2-PS1-1. Plan and conduct an investigation to describe and classify different kinds of materials by their observable properties.
	NGSS: 2-PS1-4. Construct an argument with evidence that some changes caused by heating or cooling can be reversed and some cannot.
	CCSS-ELA: SL.3.1 Engage effectively in a range of collaborative discussions (one-on-one, in groups, and teacher-led) with diverse partners on grade 3 topics and texts, building on others' ideas and expressing their own clearly.
Lesson 9: Who Stole the Principal's Water? Part II	NGSS: 2-PS1-1. Plan and conduct an investigation to describe and classify different kinds of materials by their observable properties.
	NGSS: 2-PS1-4. Construct an argument with evidence that some changes caused by heating or cooling can be reversed and some cannot.
	CCSS-ELA: SL.3.1 Engage effectively in a range of collaborative discussions (one-on-one, in groups, and teacher-led) with diverse partners on grade 3 topics and texts, building on others' ideas and expressing their own clearly.
Lesson 10: Measuring Mass	NGSS: 2-PS1-4. Construct an argument with evidence that some changes caused by heating or cooling can be reversed and some cannot.
	CCSS-Math: 3.MD.A Solve problems involving measurement and estimation.
Lesson 11: Measuring Volume	NGSS: 2-PS1-3. Make observations to construct an evidence-based account of how an object made of a small set of pieces can be disassembled and made into a new object.
	CCSS-Math: 4.MD.A Solve problems involving measurement and conversion of measurements.
	CCSS-ELA: SL.2.2 Recount or describe key ideas or details from a text read aloud or information presented orally or through other media.
Lesson 12: Evaporation Findings	NGSS: 2-PS1-4. Construct an argument with evidence that some changes caused by heating or cooling can be reversed and some cannot.
Lesson 13: Condensation	NGSS: 2-PS1-4. Construct an argument with evidence that some changes caused by heating or cooling can be reversed and some cannot.
Lesson 14: Planning the Investigation and Hosting the Matter Conference	CCSS-ELA: W.2.2 Write informative/explanatory texts in which they introduce a topic, use facts and definitions to develop points, and provide a concluding statement or section.
	CCSS-ELA: W.2.6 With guidance and support from adults, use a variety of digital tools to produce and publish writing, including in collaboration with peers.
	CCSS-ELA: W.2.8 Recall information from experiences or gather information from provided sources to answer a question.
	CCSS-ELA: W.3.2 Write informative/explanatory texts to examine a topic and convey ideas and information clearly.
	CCSS-ELA: W.3.6 With guidance and support from adults, use technology to produce and publish writing (using keyboarding skills) as well as to interact and collaborate with others.
	CCSS-ELA: SL.3.4 Report on a topic or text, tell a story, or recount an experience with appropriate facts and relevant, descriptive details, speaking clearly at an understandable pace.
Lesson 15: Concluding the Unit	CCSS-ELA: SL.2.1 Participate in collaborative conversations with diverse partners about grade 2 topics and texts with peers and adults in small and larger groups.
	CCSS-ELA: SL.3.4 Report on a topic or text, tell a story, or recount an experience with appropriate facts and relevant, descriptive details, speaking clearly at an understandable pace.